GLOBAL STRATEGIC RESPONSIVENESS

Andersen and Hallin offer a state-of-the-art and in-depth investigation of MNE global strategic responsiveness. This is a cutting edge book and must read for strategists operating in today's globalized world.
—**George O. White III**, *Old Dominion University, USA*

Global firms must operate in turbulent conditions, facing relentless pressure to be efficient, whilst also accommodating local factors and ways of thinking. This book offers an insight into how an adaptive multinational enterprise can achieve a sustainable competitive advantage in an uncertain environment.

Drawing on ground-breaking research into adaptive strategy, this book introduces compelling tools to help design responsive strategic organizations by cultivating global strategic democracy. Written by two leading scholars, this book provides models to inform strategic decisions through the aggregation of frontline information.

With a wealth of illustrative case examples supplementing unique research, this text is essential reading for students of strategic management and provides illuminating insights for the reflective practitioner.

Torben Juul Andersen is Professor of Strategy and International Management and Director of the Center for Global Strategic Responsiveness at Copenhagen Business School, Denmark.

Carina Antonia Hallin is Assistant Professor of International Business and Founder of the Collective Intelligence Unit at Copenhagen Business School, Denmark.

Strategy Matters
Edited by Thomas C. Lawton
Open University, UK and Tuck School of Business,
Dartmouth College, USA

What is strategy and does it matter? This series provides a range of concise, practical books that demonstrate the multitude of ways in which strategy matters in contemporary organizations.

Taking in cross-disciplinary approaches, the series will include books covering all of the hot topics relevant in planning and executing world-class strategies. Each book in the series will provide a unique resource for understanding a key contemporary issue facing the business world, whilst the series as a whole will provide a library for reflective practitioners and postgraduate students at MBA and Masters levels.

Global Strategic Responsiveness
Exploiting Frontline Information in the Adaptive Multinational Enterprise
Torben Juul Andersen and Carina Antonia Hallin

GLOBAL STRATEGIC RESPONSIVENESS

Exploiting Frontline Information in the Adaptive Multinational Enterprise

Torben Juul Andersen
and Carina Antonia Hallin

Routledge
Taylor & Francis Group
LONDON AND NEW YORK

First published 2017
by Routledge
2 Park Square, Milton Park, Abingdon, Oxon OX14 4RN

and by Routledge
711 Third Avenue, New York, NY 10017

Routledge is an imprint of the Taylor & Francis Group, an informa business

British Library Cataloguing-in-Publication Data
A catalogue record for this book is available from the British Library.

Library of Congress Cataloging-in-Publication Data
Names: Andersen, Torben Juul, author. | Hallin, Carina Antonia, author.
Title: Global strategic responsiveness: exploiting frontline information in the adaptive multinational enterprise / Torben Juul Andersen and Carina Antonia Hallin.
Description: Abingdon, Oxon; New York, NY: Routledge, 2017. | Includes bibliographical references and index.
Identifiers: LCCN 2016046307 | ISBN 9781138204621 (hardback) | ISBN 9781138204638 (pbk.) | ISBN 9781315469058 (ebook)
Subjects: LCSH: International business enterprises—Management. | Strategic management.
Classification: LCC HD62.4 .A464 2017 | DDC 658.4/012—dc23
LC record available at https://lccn.loc.gov/2016046307

ISBN: 978-1-138-20462-1 (hbk)
ISBN: 978-1-138-20463-8 (pbk)
ISBN: 978-1-315-46905-8 (ebk)

Typeset in Times New Roman
by codeMantra

CONTENTS

FIGURES

BOXES

PREFACE

Welcome to the *Strategy Matters* book series and I hope you enjoy the first book in our series, *Global Strategic Responsiveness* by Torben Juul Andersen and Carina Antonia Hallin.

The series title is a deliberate and dyadic play on words, as our purpose is to both explore diverse themes in strategic management and to argue that strategy remains relevant and can make a difference, even in a fast-paced world of disruption, uncertainty and transformation. As the American philosopher Henry David Thoreau noted, "it is not enough to be busy; so are the ants. The question is: what are we busy about?" Strategy, the means by which we create and take control of the future, provides direction and purpose, even, and perhaps particularly, when chaos and complexity define much of what surrounds us on a daily basis.

We created this series to connect strategy research and practice and to provide reflective practitioners with a set of rigorous, readable and relevant books on strategic management. I urge you to embrace *Global Strategic Responsiveness* and the works that follow as your very own library of leading-edge strategy volumes, written by experts in their field and applicable to challenges and opportunities you experience today or are likely to encounter tomorrow. Depending on your needs and time constraints, the series can be seen collectively as a suite of go-to reference points or individually as books that you read cover to cover and that shape how you think and act. We are particularly keen to provide tools, techniques and frameworks for doing strategy. The management thinker, Peter Drucker, once commented that, "Plans are only good intentions unless they immediately degenerate into hard work." The disconnect between strategy development and implementation defines the field and its frequent lack of legitimacy among business managers and leaders. The books in our series strive to bridge this divide and to advance processes and practices for effective strategy execution. Each book in the series provides a unique resource to understand and engage with a key contemporary strategy issue or approach. Regardless of whether you are undertaking an MBA or an MSc, pursuing executive education, or looking for an engaging read on your next long-haul flight, you will find *Strategy Matters* indispensable.

Global Strategic Responsiveness sets the tone well for the series. Andersen and Hallin's notion of the "adaptive multinational" will strike a chord with managers and leaders struggling to reconcile and respond to the requirements and restrictions of corporate headquarters with the demands and necessities on the ground in individual countries and markets. The authors observe that multinational companies, surrounded by contextual turbulence and uncertainty, face relentless pressure to be efficient (the burden of globalisation) alongside the need to accommodate local factors and insights (the necessity of localisation). Their intent is to offer new insights into how an adaptive multinational enterprise can balance these pressures to achieve sustainable competitive advantage.

Drawing on ground-breaking research into adaptive strategy, this book introduces compelling tools to help design the responsive strategic organization by cultivating global strategic democracy. The authors provide models and illustrative examples to inform strategic decisions via the aggregation of frontline information.

This book provides many novel, even radical, ideas and approaches to achieve strategic responsiveness in multinationals. In particular, the authors introduce the notion of "democratizing" the strategic engagement of multinational managers and employees as a key feature of a new leadership paradigm. In the implied *global strategic democracy*, all the critical decisions made in the responsive multinational corporation (RMC) reflect the diverse insights and views of employees and other frontline stakeholders to achieve better-informed outcomes by tapping into the crowd wisdom readily available within the organization. Hence, the RMC acknowledges the collective intelligence contributed by everyone in the organization, all of which have important insights that can be collected using information technology and exploited in conscious leadership efforts.

Through this innovative method, Andersen and Hallin connect strategy design, development and delivery, and recommend a data-driven, network-based approach and structure to engage with and reconcile the challenges and opportunities of today's multinational corporations. Global strategic democracy can exploit global efficiencies and enable local responsiveness by leveraging the interconnected domains of information, communication and technology and embedding these in organisational networks. The authors further argue that blending a *fast* and *slow* approach to strategy (fast in responding to business imperatives at a local level and slow in charting the longer-term, forward-looking plans at headquarters level), facilitated by information and communication technology, creates an adaptive dynamic system that forges strategic response capabilities which render the corporation more resilient and agile. The ability to orchestrate an effective responsive dynamic in a multinational depends on corporate norms and values that support open communication and collaboration.

This book will provoke and stimulate your thinking about strategy and structure in multinationals, and cause you to reflect on the connectivity between information, communication and collaboration in how you design and implement strategy for international business. I sincerely hope that you find *Global Strategic Responsiveness* informative and insightful and that you are encouraged to engage further with *Strategy Matters* as the series progresses.

Professor Thomas C. Lawton
Series Editor

1

EFFECTIVE MULTINATIONAL RESPONSES COMBINING INTENDED AND EMERGENT ACTIONS

Key points

- Advantages of central and decentralized processes
- Increasing responsiveness from interactive strategy-making
- Consequences of disconnected fast and slow processes
- Using information from the global frontline

The global business environment is often characterized as being highly dynamic and complex with frequent economic, political and technological changes taking place across interdependent national and regional market spheres. These turbulent conditions are associated with fundamental uncertainty where various hazards, economic, political and social conflicts are difficult to predict and foresee (Bettis and Hitt, 1995). In this context successful multinational organizations must have effective strategic response capabilities and collaborative learning mechanisms in place to adapt to frequent and potentially abrupt changes in the global business environment. The key to creating these conditions for success is to establish an organizational dynamic of interacting fast and slow strategy-making processes that combine decentralized responses with central forward-looking analytics supported by open information systems within a culture of collaborative learning.

Contemporary competitive contexts have been referred to as *hyper-competitive* where frequent technological changes and continuous ongoing innovation challenge the competitive advantages of incumbent firms (e.g., D'Aveni, 2010; McGrath, 2013). In these environmental settings, strategic response capabilities (Bettis and Hitt, 1995), adaptive capabilities (Volberda, 1996) and dynamic capabilities (Teece et al., 1997) become essential as the means to attain sustainable performance. These conditions require that the organization is able to process large amounts of specialized information across diverse knowledge-based competencies dispersed among many individuals in and outside the organization (Child and McGrath, 2001). Hence, it is argued that organizations can increase their responsiveness by moving decision authority to the local business entities where the relevant operational information and expertise resides (Daft and Lewin, 1993). However, to make this work successfully the decentralized emergent responses must be enhanced without foregoing the ability of integrating business activities to gain economic efficiencies and work towards common goals.

To this end the communication enhancing capacity of new information technologies can serve as a facilitating mechanism to enable efficient coordination of both planned and more spontaneous responsive efforts dealing with turbulent global market conditions (Andersen, 2001; Andersen and Segars, 2001). The use of communication and information technologies (CIT) can support both formal and informal exchanges of knowledge across internal networks as well as link internal agents to external knowledge communities that extend well beyond the confines of the organization. The more formal, structured and preprogrammed use of CIT both across internal and external networks can improve productivity and increase economic efficiencies. The informal autonomous and more spontaneous use of CIT where knowledge is exchanged freely across networks of many individuals can facilitate creativity and innovation in the appropriate organizational settings. It can also improve economic outcomes under highly turbulent market conditions because it enables open thinking about solutions to unpredictable developments through collaborative learning involving many knowledgeable actors, which leads to more effective outcomes in the face of changing circumstances (Andersen, 2001, 2005).

The ability to create value across international markets with ethnic, religious and cultural diversity with access to natural resources, production, services and new technologies calls for effective multinational strategy-making processes (Andersen, 2013). The multinational organization must be resilient against major economic and political events and retain the flexibility to identify, develop and exploit opportunities that draw on local resources, market knowledge and innovative capacity (Berry, 2006, 2014; Kogut and Kulatilaka, 1994; Kogut and Zander, 1992). It depends on an ability to take informed strategic decisions that enable the organization to respond to emerging risks and opportunities in local markets and adapt business activities in ways that are in sync with the changing environmental conditions (Andersen and Bettis, 2015; Andersen et al., 2007). This entails effective ways to utilize market intelligence collected from local stakeholders for immediate responsive actions and as informative input to the central forward-looking strategic-thinking process at headquarters (Hallin et al., 2013; Hallin and Lind, 2016).

A resilient multinational organization that can withstand exogenous influences and at the same time exploit comparative advantages across diverse turbulent market settings must respond with corrective actions informed by updated local market intelligence considering the long-term strategic consequences. This responsive organization will depend on an effective strategy-making process across multinational business entities informed by updated market information obtained from local stakeholders processed through the intermediation of effective global communication systems.

A multinational presence promises access to many diverse resources, insights and revenue models that can support innovation and new business development across the firm but will expose the multinational organization in new unprecedented ways (Doukas and Kan, 2006; Gupta and Govindarajan, 2001). Hence, the multinational organization should take advantage of knowledge-based resources that can be transferred at low cost and locate capital-intensive production facilities within flexible resilient global structures. That is, the multinational organization must be able to access and utilize local resources and knowledge on a global scale while maintaining a flexible production and distribution platform that is resistant to many types of exogenous events and circumstances. There is a need for an effective multinational decision structure that combines local responses with central planning considerations supported by management control processes where ongoing strategic decisions are informed by updated insights from local stakeholders. This implies that it should be possible to take decentralized initiatives as local conditions change and coordinate corporate business activities centrally to gain economic efficiencies.

It is important to balance local responses with the ability to optimize global operations in the internationalizing firms that are exposed to turbulent global market conditions (Andersen, 2004a, 2004b; Andersen and Foss, 2005). We know that the corporate decisions must be executed effectively at different hierarchical levels and across geographical locations where IT-enhanced processing of strategic information is a prerequisite for the ability to facilitate adaptive strategic decisions. The ability to balance local decentralized decisions with central forward-looking planning considerations in a multinational organization represents the recipe for effective strategy-making across a dispersed portfolio of business activities located in diverse turbulent local markets (Andersen, 2013). However, the generic interactive strategy-making model must be refined to suit the multinational context with communication and information-processing capabilities linking decision makers in geographically dispersed markets.

Favorable risk–return outcomes among multinational organizations seem to derive from a delicate balance between the ability to respond locally across the national markets and maintain an interactive IT-enhanced decision-making capacity around the corporate center (Andersen, 2004a, 2004b; Andersen and Foss, 2005; Andersen and Nielsen, 2009). Hence, the ability to create value across markets with ethnic, religious and cultural differences, access to diverse resources, products, services and technologies, depends on effective multinational strategy-making processes (Andersen, 2013). A complex multinational firm that operates across highly diverse and turbulent markets can thrive from collective learning and innovative responses fueled by local market insights. In contrast, executives confined at the center of corporate headquarters may tend to develop dominant logics (Bettis and Prahalad, 1995) where the adoption of specific management styles will affect performance (Sax and Torp, 2015). In this context, recent research finds that CEO humbleness and humility (Ou et al., 2014) have a positive effect on performance whereas narcissism (e.g., Chatterjee and Hambrick, 2007) and hubris (Li and Tang, 2013) have an adverse effect on the ability to engage local knowledge in collective learning for innovation.

Central and decentralized processes

The conventional depiction of strategic management is a sequential process of analytics-based planning activities, subsequent execution of business plans and monitoring of performance outcomes in regular diagnostic control processes. The planning considerations can be influenced by managerial concerns and environmental perceptions trying to interpret the competitive reality and plan strategic actions that can address the emerging conditions effectively. The dynamic view of the formal strategic planning process is comprised by *ex ante* environmental analyses, considering strategic alternatives, and choosing a strategic path to execute and update action plans based on information from *ex post* evaluations of realized outcomes (e.g., Schendel and Hofer, 1979). This traditional view assumes that a central administration around top management at headquarters conducts environmental analyses and outlines a path of strategic actions for subsequent implementation. These planning activities, that typically fall within an annual process, establish the strategic direction, set long- and medium-term goals and outline key activities to be implemented across the organization. However, when environmental conditions change, local managers at the frontline of the organization must be able to react to new situations imposed by observed changes. As these responsive actions are effectuated over time, their cumulative effects on performance are registered in the periodic budget reports as realized strategic outcomes.

There is general agreement that local innovative responses and entrepreneurial behaviors are essential to uncover opportunities that can renew the strategy in view of emerging changes in the environment. However, there is also mounting evidence that rationality and structure are important to secure economic efficiency across globally dispersed business activities (e.g., Baum and Wally, 2003; Brews and Hunt, 1999; Goll and Rasheed, 1997). Hence, effective adaptive strategies for the multinational organization will rely on integrative structures that allow dispersed decision makers to explore local opportunities and integrate the updated insights from these experiences in the central planning process at headquarters (Figure 1.1).

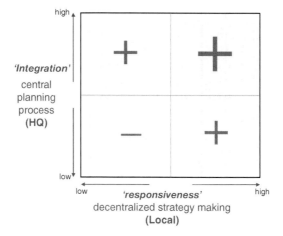

FIGURE 1.1   Interactive central-decentralized strategy-making.

Hence, firms that are able to pursue both integration through a central planning process at headquarters and local responsiveness through decentralized strategy-making will generally outperform their peers in the industry whereas those that can do neither will lose out (Andersen, 2000, 2004a, 2004b). An example of a company that successfully pursued the integration of local responsiveness is Hewlett Packard of the 1990s. As the company grew, they realized that the business activities had to be structured for efficiency while at the same time avoiding the perils of centralization. Hence, they disbanded the business executive committees and gave more freedom to the operating units to make their own decisions, thereby creating a more flexible and agile organization (Packard, 1995). The positive effects of a central planning process combined with decentralized strategy-making are particularly pronounced in turbulent industry contexts characterized by such highly dynamic and complex business environments as those faced by internationalizing firms. That is, firms with a higher degree of international business activities will benefit from interactive central-decentralized strategy-making.

The dual concern for integration and distributed entrepreneurship has also been expressed as a balance between exploitation and exploration (March, 1991), calling for organizational *ambidexterity* (e.g., O'Reilly and Tushman, 2008). In strategy, similar perspectives have been referred to as *intended* and *emergent* strategies (Mintzberg, 1978; Mintzberg and Waters, 1985), *induced* and *autonomous* strategies (Burgelman and Grove, 1996, 2007) and *central* planning and *decentralized* decision-making (Andersen, 2004a, 2004b; Andersen and Nielsen, 2009). These views imply that effective multinational organizations have top managers at headquarters actively involved in the strategy-making process but at the same time give local managers in the national markets sufficient decision-making power to respond and create important insights as potential reconnaissance for the strategic planning considerations.

Based on a simple two-by-two framework, we can identify four strategy typologies as determined by the relative emphasis on central reasoning (planning) and decentralized initiatives (autonomous responses) (Figure 1.2). This produces four quadrants of "visioning" (I), "reasoning" (II), "responding" (III), and "interacting" (IV) (Andersen, 2015). *Visioning* reflects organizations that neither plan nor respond but rather take their lead from the great vision of a central leader who sets the direction for the firm. *Reasoning* represents organizations that engage headquarter executives and key decision makers throughout the firm in forward-looking analytics-based planning considerations to assess the future direction. *Responding* corresponds to organizations where local managers have authority to respond to emerging situations without any influence from headquarters. *Interacting* depicts organizations that combine central planning activities at headquarters with distributed decision authority, which allows local managers to respond and take actions in view of changing conditions. A typical representative of an interacting organization is Hewlett-Packard as it operated in the 1980s and 90s with a strong sense of direction and values as a central structure but with broad autonomy to take independent initiatives and innovate in view of emerging market opportunities. The interacting typology is high performing because

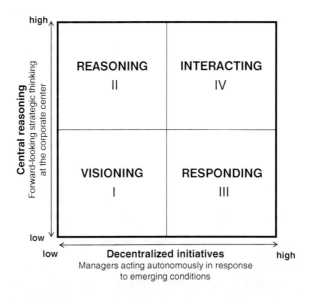

FIGURE 1.2 Variations in central and local strategy-making processes.

it allows fast local responses to changing conditions that create valuable current insights to be considered in the long-term strategic planning. This mix of central and local processes assumes the active engagement of top management at the corporate headquarters as well as geographically dispersed local managers that are linked together through open exchange of information. The exchange of information can also make active use of mechanisms to collect updated insights from stakeholders around the local subsidiaries for consideration in the central strategy-making process at the headquarters.

Interacting strategy-making

The analytical reasoning performed at headquarters around the forward-looking strategic thinking of the corporate leadership is a *slow*, time-consuming process of trying to reconcile the global competitive environment and consider future strategic alternatives by simulating possible outcomes. The decentralized initiatives taken by local managers represent fast processes that respond to the immediate changes taking place in the surrounding business environment. This modus operandi resembles the cognitive processes of the human brain that seems to operate through complementary fast and slow processes (Kahneman, 2011). The fast system responds to changes in the surroundings and observes the outcomes from ongoing interactions between the body and the environment more or less automatically. The slow system is a conscious activity that tries to interpret the various outcomes from interactions with the surroundings and consider the way to move forward by reasoning. This interplay between brain, body and the environment can be juxtaposed to the organizational processes where decentralized actors respond to immediate influences and observe reactions where central processes of reasoning plan alternative paths forward in the changing environment. The changing conditions are observed in the fast system and the slow system interprets the observations and reasons about the future direction. These dual processes are discussed in the management literature. For example, fast responses correspond to experience-based "on-line" decision-making that creates new insights from trial-and-error learning whereas the slow planning system corresponds to forward-looking analytical assessments from simulated calculations in "off-line" reasoning (e.g., Gavetti and Levinthal, 2000).

The central planning process at headquarters constitutes a learning loop that we can refer to as *strategic learning*. It is long-cycled because each of the planning iterations with the associated budget follow-up reporting takes time (Figure 1.3). However, it constitutes a learning process in the sense that the management reports periodically compare realized outcomes with the intended outcomes that were planned, so as to understand the reasons for possible discrepancies and assess the need for corrective actions. The ongoing actions taken by local (middle) managers also represent learning loops that we can refer to as *experiential learning*, as the results observed from each of the autonomous initiatives taken in response to emerging changes give new insights. Since these responsive actions are taken on an ongoing basis they are short-cycled. It is this combination of slow long-cycled planning processes and the fast short-cycled responsive actions that make up the interactive strategy-making process where learning takes place through the exchange of current experiential insights and forward-looking reasoning, fueled by lots of informal communication among engaged actors at all management levels, in all business functions, and in all the geographical locations.

The slow planning and control process can engage in discussions with key people at headquarters and in local business entities, as the means to develop a shared understanding of the competitive landscape and form a sensible strategic direction going forward. The involvement of decision makers from different parts of the organization can facilitate a shared cognition across a diverse set of constituents with different functional expertise and market experiences. So, the planning exercise can consider different opinions and shape a common understanding of the competitive situation with implied guidance to updated strategic decisions (e.g., Hendry, 2000). The combination of fast and slow processes can stimulate a *dynamic* system that enhances the organization's ability to take timely responses, interact, and adapt the strategic direction. An integrated structure that combines experiential insights from dispersed actions and central cognition from forward-looking reasoning constitutes such a dynamic system that forms the organization's strategic response capabilities.

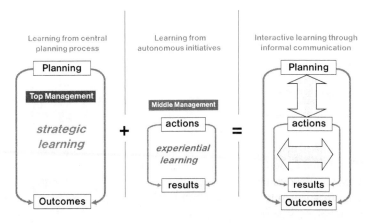

FIGURE 1.3 Combining central planning and autonomous actions.

BOX 1.1 Responding effectively to global strategic issues

The ability to establish a dynamic system for global strategic responsiveness is probably worth considering for any multinational organization and it turns out that the presence of heterogeneous strategic response capabilities across all international firms in a given industry can explain the observed inverse risk–return relationships. That is, the ability to install strategic response capabilities is generally associated with higher average returns and lower performance risk at the same time. Assuming that effective strategic response capabilities are reflected in low variation in performance outcomes over time where adverse events are deflected and opportunities gradually developed then low variance is associated with high average returns in a given industry, say computer products (Figure 1.4).

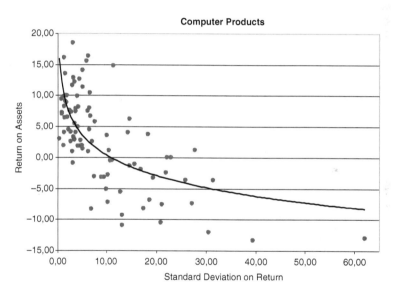

FIGURE 1.4   The inverse risk–return relationship in the international computer products industry.

Source: large public firms included in the Compustat database over the period 1991–2000.

We consider steady business performance as a good indicator of effective response capabilities as it supposedly helps the organization deal with emerging threats and opportunities as they arise in a turbulent global market context in a way that avoids extreme outcomes following a steady adaptive course. Potential events are identified and handled properly, so no incidents should dent the earnings development at least compared to the close competitors in the industry that operate under the same competitive conditions. Hence, the ability to avoid major losses and manage opportunities helps the international organization adapt to ongoing environmental changes and as a consequence the earnings development is more stable and less erratic as reflected in low variability in performance outcomes compared to peers in the same industry.

The claim that effective strategic response capabilities can derive from superior management conduct is illustrated by a simple *strategic responsiveness model* expressed in a performance function that reflects the ability to respond, and adapt the international organization to ongoing environmental changes (Andersen et al., 2007). An underlying assumption is that organizations in practice display different adaptive capabilities, where some respond better to changing conditions than others. This assumption is quite consistent with the evidence. One only has to read the headlines of major newspapers on a regular basis to note various corporate scandals that illustrate the point. Firms perform well when they are able to adapt their business activities and operational structure to match changes in environmental conditions. To enable this, actors in the firm must observe and respond to the changes to find viable solutions that can restructure the firm and adapt it to the observed changes. As discussed above this kind of adaptive capability may be achieved by a dynamic system combining decentralized responses with central forward-looking reasoning.

A simple way to model this is to look at the economic resources available to the multinational organization that can achieve a maximum performance outcome if existing technologies are used properly. This optimum performance level is expressed as value K, but it can only be achieved if the company can set up its business activities as a perfect match to the requirements demanded by the global environmental conditions. The ability to assess the environment and respond to accurately match the changes will lead to high performance outcomes over time. If a company is unable to assess the emerging changes and respond properly it will perform below the optimum level. The performance function (P) of a given firm in period t as a function of its ability to adapt can be expressed as:

$$P_t = K - b|c_t - d_t|^a$$

In this model c_t can be interpreted as a key parameter in the environment, for example, total demand, customer needs, technology choice, or the like, whereas d_t is the corresponding decision variable indicating the firm's chosen position on that parameter at time t. Managers observe environmental changes and redeploy resources towards solutions that can adapt the firm so it obtains a better match with the environment. The model coefficients a and b are assumed positive, so deviations from a perfect fit between firm position and the environment ($d_t \neq c_t$) will lead to lower performance where the coefficients determine the severity of the performance loss.

If the multinational organization is unable to match the global environment, performance will suffer in proportion to the size of the discrepancy between the firm position and the environment ($|c_t - d_{t-1}|$). Several manage-rial challenges illustrate this. For example, performance suffers if the firm is unable to estimate demand and inventory builds up, or if a wrong technology is used that renders the product uncompetitive. Performance can also be affected if service is excessive or insufficient, if the level of advertising is too high or too low, and so forth.

Even though the adaptation process is likely to impose some costs, the performance of multinational organizations with different strategic response capabilities will lead to an inverse risk–return relationship because the respon-sive firms achieve better fit and thus higher performance and lower variation in outcomes over time. And indeed this is the phenomenon one observes when analyzing performance outcomes, or financial returns, across interna-tional firms in given industries.

So, multinational organizations that can perfectly match the changing global business environment over time will realize better performance and show lower variation in performance from period to period. That is, highly re-sponsive and adaptive firms display significantly better risk–return outcomes.

This can easily be applied to an extended multinational organization with operations in multiple locations around the world. In this case the general strate-gic responsiveness model can consider multiple (m) global risk factors that may affect the firm (see Appendix). The performance function (P) of the multinational organization in period t as a function of m parameters can be expressed as:

$$R_t = K - \sum b|c_{m,t} - d_{m,t}|^a - \sum C_{m,t}; \; t = 1, 2, 3 \ldots T; \; m = 1, 2, 3 \ldots M$$

Now we just take more multinational environmental conditions into account but the outcome of the exercise is still the same as before. That is, those multi-national organizations that are able to observe, respond, and adapt to the major global risk factors that expose the global business environment will outperform and display favorable inverse risk–return outcomes with higher average return and lower variation in outcomes compared to peers in the industry.

Disconnected fast and slow processes

In humans, an imbalance in favor of the slow system can lead to mental dis-eases (McGilchrist, 2009). When the fast system fails to feed ongoing impres-sions into the slow system of reasoning a person can become schizophrenic with symptoms of hyperconsciousness and abstract thinking without a foundation in reality. Changes in the surrounding environment are played down, whereas the static and controllable aspects take the center stage.

Strategic management perceived as a central process of planning, exe-cution and monitoring often sees decisions confined to top management that consequently may preclude them from receiving updated experiential insights from different parts of the organization. If this is the case we may discern organizational symptoms that resemble schizophrenia among humans. Hence, it is important to combine the central forward-looking planning and control features with an ongoing ability to learn from updated experiential insights derived from decentralized responsive actions taken in view of changing conditions. That is, central planning activities should incorporate experiential learning from decentralized actions (e.g., Andersen, 2004a, 2004b; Andersen and Nielsen, 2009; Brews and Hunt, 1999).

A network of individuals in an organization comprising both central and decentralized decision makers constitutes the core of a dynamic system of slow and fast processes. The immediate surroundings are interpreted based on observed experiences from responsive actions taken by locally dispersed managers and the corporate understanding of the environment evolves from central analytical forward-looking considerations informed by these updated insights. We may refer to this as an *organizational mind*, as conceptualized by the strategic plan that is being updated and revised from experiential learning that takes place from decentralized actions taken in response to changes in the real world.

If the information updating of top management at headquarters nonetheless becomes biased due to limited access to insights from local experiments, the environmental context will increasingly be interpreted on the basis of historical experiences that gradually become irrelevant. The potentially disastrous effects caused by cognitive biases among senior executives are well described and can arise when they become disconnected from the daily business activities (e.g., Bazerman and Moore, 2008). The resulting environmental misperceptions may also explain organizational inertia (e.g., Hannan and Freeman, 1989) and the limitations of *dominant logics* (Bettis and Prahalad, 1995) when executives make decisions based on prior successful experiences that no longer apply.

Corporate norms and values

In multinational organizations norms and values embedded in the corporate culture will influence the way people think and behave. The traits of regional and national cultures also influence the way people reason and act together. Culture is a part of human actions, as we are shaped by the culture of the social networks we operate in and that subscribe to certain rules and behavioral norms. The collective cognitive capabilities imposed around this network behavior can develop a distinct mode of conduct reflected in particular abilities to respond to and deal with changes in the environment.

A network of individuals forms a collective intelligence with no formal control center and it has emergent non-linear properties that can be updated from current insights in the presence of behavioral norms that are conducive to collaborative learning (Kauffman, 1993). Hence, creativity and innovative behavior depends on a supportive organizational culture with surroundings where the individuals receive proper encouragements to interact and learn, together with other individuals in the network. The communication links comprise both exchanges between internal actors as well as exchanges between internal and external actors in different overseas markets (Figure 1.5).

The internal communication links can serve as an informal means to co-ordinate mutually dependent activities whenever new initiatives are taken and it can also serve as the vehicle to exchange knowledge and new insights that further organizational learning, challenging current interpretations to find new ways of understanding the business context. The external communication links can serve as a simple means to access information from a broad contingent of outside (global) sources and can facilitate *absorptive capacity* to the extent that external experiences can be observed and interpreted for inclusion in ways that enhance their own processes (Cohen and Levinthal, 1990). The communication links that tie internal actors together and provide access to external sources of information obviously become increasingly important as the firm internationalizes its business activities across multiple national environments.

Learning together in a network of individuals requires a setting where those individuals can interact within a supportive social system with an ability to communicate current observations and exchange new insights. The underlying cultural norms are formed by information that affects individual behaviors and arises from organizational learning processes where information stored in individual brains is exchanged across a social system (Boyd and Richerson, 2005). Culture is information exchanged among individuals in social transmission mechanisms constituted by knowledge, skills,

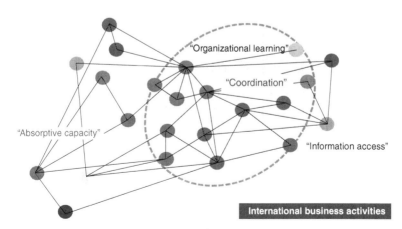

FIGURE 1.5 Communication links between individuals in and around the organization.

experiences, beliefs, attitudes, preferences and norms stored collectively in the individual brains.

The combination of fast and slow systems where individuals interact within a network can be tied together by an organizational culture as a social corporate fabric that is both efficient and effective in dealing with uncertain business conditions and unpredictable emerging developments in the global competitive environment.

Effective responsiveness in a multinational organization exposed to the turbulence of global markets will rely on a setting that is conducive to collaborative learning among networked individuals. This setting is defined by cultural norms, attitudes and expectations that can encourage and inspire interaction and ongoing discussions among individuals in all parts of the organization. This includes exchanges about experiential insights from responsive actions to emerging changes as the information is communicated and exchanged among individuals at different local business units and at headquarters. In this context, it is important to encourage local communication as well as enable links across different knowledge communities and to the central planning functions when dealing with complex strategic issues. Hence, the internal communication links should both comprise *horizontal* channels across functional and geographical entities as well as *vertical* channels up and down the hierarchy between top management at headquarters and local managers with functional responsibilities (Figure 1.6).

The *horizontal* communication links can exchange updated insights and specialized knowledge across many individuals located in different functional entities and geographical locations to facilitate collaborative

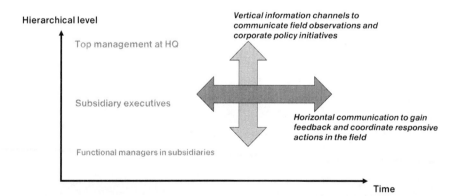

FIGURE 1.6 Internal communication links across hierarchies and between business units.

learning and informal coordination of mutually dependent corporate business activities. The *vertical* information channels can serve as the means to communicate important field observations and experiential insights to higher-level managers from individuals throughout the organization. It can also be used to facilitate open corporate communication around current management information reports with important news on corporate policy initiatives.

There is a need for local observance and fast responses in the local operational entities as well as for analytical evaluations of future solutions around top management at headquarters. One should not go without the other. The essential leadership challenge is to enable this dynamic system in an organizational structure that can support both fast and slow processes with communication and information systems to facilitate the necessary interaction. The multinational executive assumes an important role of enabling an effective strategy-making dynamic around a corporate culture that is supportive of human interaction and collaborative learning.

The dynamic system between interacting fast and slow strategy-making processes can ensure that environmental changes are observed and responded to on an ongoing basis through the fast system of dispersed empowered managers in the local markets. The insights gained from these responsive actions can serve as needed information to fuel collaborative learning among many individuals throughout the multinational organization to facilitate better solutions to emerging challenges. Effective communication channels must be in place to ensure that key observations are exchanged and possible solutions brought to the attention of the slow analytical process of corporate strategizing.

The dispersion of decision-making power ensures that local managers can take exploratory initiatives, closer to the overseas markets, which may uncover new business opportunities. The strategic management process with related control systems at headquarters can be used for forward-looking evaluations of strategic opportunities derived from this dispersed reconnaissance.

This requires structure, processes, systems and cultural traits that enhance a dynamic based on interacting fast and slow processes with decentralized responses and experimentation, collective learning to find viable solutions, and an organizational culture to incorporate them in central forward-looking analyses. The implication for multinational organizations is that the cognition of top management matters and must be updated by actively involving collaborative learning efforts across diverse individuals in different locations, functions and hierarchical positions. It implies that a primary leadership role is to instill responsive behaviors with organizational structures and systems to facilitate local experimentation and collective learning, submitting possible solutions to the scrutiny of central planning.

Summary

Interacting strategy-making between central planning processes at corporate headquarters and decentralized responsiveness at local business entities facilitated by IT-enhanced communication and information technology is the essence of a dynamic adaptive system that forms the strategic response capabilities. This adaptive dynamic is particularly useful for multinational organizations operating in a turbulent global business environment and it is associated with favorable risk–return outcomes. The ability to orchestrate an effective responsive dynamic in a multinational organization depends on corporate norms and values that support open communication and collaboration.

References

Andersen, T. J. (2000). Strategic planning, autonomous actions and corporate performance. *Long Range Planning*, **33**: 184–200.

Andersen, T. J. (2001). Information technology, strategic decision making approaches and organizational performance in different industrial settings. *Journal of Strategic Information Systems*, **30**: 101–119.

Andersen, T. J. (2004a). Integrating decentralized strategy making and strategic planning processes in dynamic environments. *Journal of Management Studies*, **41**(8): 1271–1299.

Andersen, T. J. (2004b). Integrating the strategy formation process: An international perspective. *European Management Journal*, **22**(3): 263–272.

Andersen T. J. (2005). The performance effect of computer-mediated communication and decentralized strategic decision making. *Journal of Business Research*, **58**: 1059–1067.

Andersen, T. J. (2013). *Short Introduction to Strategic Management*. Cambridge, UK: Cambridge University Press.

Andersen, T. J. (2015). Interactive strategy-making: Combining central reasoning with ongoing learning from decentralized responses. *Journal of General Management*, **40**(4): 69–88.

Andersen, T. J. and Bettis, R. A. (2015). Exploring longitudinal risk-return relationships. *Strategic Management Journal*, **36**(8): 1135–1145.

Andersen, T. J. and Foss, N. J. (2005). Strategic opportunity and economic performance in multinational enterprises: The role and effects of information and communication technology. *Journal of International Management*, **11**(2): 293–310.

Andersen, T. J. and Nielsen, B. B. (2009). Adaptive strategy making: The effects of emergent and intended strategy modes. *European Management Review*, **6**(2): 94–106.

Andersen, T. J. and Segars, A. H. (2001). The impact of IT on decision structure and firm performance: Evidence from the textile and apparel industry. *Information & Management*, **39**: 85–100.

Andersen, T. J., Denrell, J. and Bettis, R. A. (2007). Strategic Responsiveness and Bowman's Risk-Return Paradox. *Strategic Management Journal*, **28**: 407–429.

Baum, J. and Wally, S. (2003). Strategic decision speed and firm performance. *Strategic Management Journal*, **24**(11): 1107–1129.

Bazerman, M. H. and Moore, D. A. (2008). *Judgment in Managerial Decision Making*. Hoboken, NJ: Wiley.

Berry, H. (2006). Leaders, laggards, and the pursuit of foreign knowledge. *Strategic Management Journal*, **27**(2): 151–168.

Berry, H. (2014). Global integration and innovation: Multicountry knowledge generation within MNCs. *Strategic Management Journal*, **35**(6): 869–890.

Bettis, R. A. and Hitt, M. A. (1995). The new competitive landscape. *Strategic management Journal*, **16**(S1): 7–19.

Bettis, R. A. and Prahalad, C. K. (1995). The dominant logic: Retrospective and extension. *Strategic Management Journal*, **16**(1): 5–14.

Boyd, R. and Richerson, P. J. (2005). *The Origin and Evolution of Cultures*. New York, NY: Oxford University Press.

Brews, P. J. and Hunt, M. R. (1999). Learning to plan and planning to learn: Resolving the planning school/learning school debate. *Strategic Management Journal*, **20**: 889–913.

Burgelman, R. A. and Grove, A. S. (1996). Strategic dissonance. *California Management Review*, **38**(2): 8–28.

Burgelman, R. A. and Grove, A. S. (2007). Let chaos reign, then rein in chaos—repeatedly: Managing strategic dynamics for corporate longevity. *Strategic Management Journal*, **28**(10): 965–979.

Chatterjee, A. and Hambrick, D. C. (2007). It's all about me: Narcissistic chief executive officers and their effects on company strategy and performance. *Administrative Science Quarterly*, **52**(3): 351–386.

Child, J. and McGrath, R. G. (2001). Organizations unfettered: Organizational form in an information-intensive economy. *Academy of Management Journal*, **44**(6): 1135–1148.

Cohen, W. M. and Levinthal, D. A. (1990). Absorptive capacity: A new perspective on learning and innovation. *Administrative Science Quarterly*, **35**: 128–152.

Daft, R. L. and Lewin, A. Y. (1993). Where are the theories for the "new" organizational forms? An editorial essay. *Organization Science*, i–vi.

D'aveni, R. A. (2010). *Hypercompetition*. New York, NY: Simon and Schuster.

Doukas, J. A. and Kan, O. B. (2006). Does global diversification destroy firm value? *Journal of International Business Studies*, **37**(3): 352–371.

Gavetti, G. and Levinthal, D. (2000). Looking forward and looking backward: Cognitive and experiential search. *Administrative Science Quarterly*, **45**(1): 113–137.

Goll, I. and Rasheed, A. M. (1997). Rational decision-making and firm performance: The moderating role of environment. *Strategic Management Journal*, **18**: 583–591.

Gupta, A. K. and Govindarajan, V. (2004). *Global Strategy and Organization*. New York: Wiley.

Hallin, C. A. and Lind, A. S. (2016). Strategic issue identification for crowd predictions. Paper presented at Collective Intelligence 2016, New York.

Hallin, C. A., Andersen, T. J. and Tveterås, S. (2013). Fuzzy Predictions for Strategic Decision Making: A Third-Generation Prediction Market. Frederiksberg: Copenhagen Business School [wp], 2013. (CGSR Working Paper Series; Nr. 2.)

Hannan, M. T. and Freeman, J. (1989). *Organization Ecology*. Boston, MA: Harvard University Press.

Hendry, J. (2000). Strategic decision making, discourse, and strategy as social practice. *Journal of Management Studies*, **37**(7): 955–978.

Kahneman, D. (2011). *Thinking, Fast and Slow*. New York, NY: Macmillan.

Kauffman, S. A. (1993). *The Origins of Order: Self Organization and Selection in Evolution*. New York, NY: Oxford University Press.

Kogut, B. and Kulatilaka, N. (1994). Operating flexibility, global manufacturing, and the option value of a multinational network. *Management Science*, **40**(1): 123–139.

Kogut, B. and Zander, U. (1992). Knowledge of the firm, combinative capabilities, and the replication of technology. *Organization Science*, 3(3): 383–397.

Li, J. T. and Tang, Y. (2013). The social influence of executive hubris: Cross-cultural comparison and indigenous factors. *Management International Review*, **53**: 83–107.

March, J. G. (1991). Exploration and exploitation in organizational learning. *Organization Science*, **2**(1): 71–87.

McGilchrist, I. (2009). *The Master and His Emissary: The Divided Brain and the Making of the Western World*. New Haven, CT: Yale University Press.

McGrath, R. G. (2013). *The End of Competitive Advantage: How to Keep Your Strategy Moving as Fast as Your Business*. Boston, MA: Harvard Business Review Press.

Mintzberg, H. (1978). Patterns in strategy formation. *Management Science*, **24**(9): 934–948.

Mintzberg, H. and Waters, J. A. (1985). Of strategies, deliberate and emergent, *Strategic Management Journal*, **6**(3): 257–272.

O'Reilly, C. A. and Tushman, M. L. (2008). Ambidexterity as a dynamic capability: Resolving the innovator's dilemma. *Research in Organizational Behavior*, **28**: 185–206.

Ou, A. Y., Tsui, A. S., Kinicki, A. J., Waldman, D. A., Xiao, Z. and Song, L. J. (2014). Humble chief executive officers' connections to top management team integration and middle managers' responses. *Administrative Science Quarterly*, **59**(1): 34–72.

Packard, D. (1995). *The HP Way: How Bill Hewlett and I Built Our Company*. New York, NY: HarperCollins.

Sax, J. and Torp, S. S. (2015). Speak up! Enhancing risk performance with enterprise risk management, leadership style and employee voice. *Management Decision*, **53**(7): 1452–1468.

Schendel, D. and Hofer, C. W. (eds.) (1979). *Strategic Management: A New View of Business Policy and Planning*. New York , NY: Little, Brown.

Teece, D. J., Pisano, G. and Shuen, A. (1997). Dynamic capabilities and strategic management. *Strategic Management Journal*, **18**: 509–533.

Volberda, H. W. (1996). Toward the flexible form: How to remain vital in hypercompetitive environments. *Organization Science*, **7**(4): 359–374.

Appendix

A. General strategic responsiveness model

$$P_t = K - b|c_t - d_t|^a - C_t$$

where;

P_t = Performance for the firm in period "t"

K = Maximum possible performance with existing technology and industry structure

c_t = State of the environment on an essential strategic parameter, or risk factor, at time "t"

d_t = Actual position of the firm on the strategic parameter, or risk factor, at time "t"

$|c_t - d_t|$ = The mismatch between the environment and the firm at time "t"

a, b = Coefficients that determine the penalty for misfit, where $a \geq 1$ and $b > 0$

C_t = Costs of adaptation in period "t" that are proportional to the size of change $[C_t = f|d_t - d_{t-1}|]$

B. Extended strategic responsiveness model

The general strategic responsiveness model can be extended to consider multiple (m) multinational strategic parameters or global risk factors in each period, e.g., $d_{1,t}, d_{2,t}, d_{3,t}, \ldots d_{m,t}$,

$$R_t = K - \sum b|c_{m,t} - d_{m,t}|^a - \sum C_{m,t}; t = 1, 2, 3 \ldots T; m = 1, 2, 3 \ldots M$$

The number of strategic parameters or risk factors (m) to consider can in principle be as large as one wants to consider. The consequence for the total model is the same. Firms that are able to adapt on as many of the identified parameter and risk factors as possible will outperform their peers and display favorable risk–return outcomes.

In practice, however, the focus on major strategic parameters and risk factors will not exceed a range between 5 and 10 ($5 \leq M \leq 10$) simply because individual managers cannot handle an excessive number of parameters at the same time due to the cognitive limitations of the human brain.

2

THE DUAL PRESSURES FOR INTEGRATION AND RESPONSIVENESS

Key points

- International business strategy
- Global integration and local responsiveness
- Multinational corporate strategy considerations

A conventional view on multinational strategy-making depicts a rational analytical forward-looking process of reasoning at the corporate headquarters to find a proper strategic direction for the enterprise (Anthony, 1965; Schendel and Hofer, 1979). Forward-looking strategic planning is used to assess the competitive conditions and choose between alternative strategic paths to accomplish long-term corporate goals and guide the execution of those intended aims. This may entail discussions among the executives in the multinational organization, involving managers with functional, business and local market responsibilities to develop a shared understanding of the overarching strategic aims specifying the corporate actions needed to reach them. As discussed in the previous chapter a realistic depiction of this complex strategy-making process in a multinational organization will embrace both *intended* (planned) and *emergent* activities that respond to changing business conditions.

Numerous studies have demonstrated how the ability to facilitate emergent autonomous business initiatives can turn into highly significant and important strategic options for the corporation (e.g., Burgelman, 1983; Burgelman and Grove, 1996). Other studies have shown how many decisions made throughout the organization can be the true source to competence development that eventually determine which business opportunities a corporation is able to pursue (e.g., Bower, 1970; Noda and Bower, 1996). Many resource-committing decisions are delegated to managers throughout the multinational organization at lower hierarchical levels, even though the formal capital budgeting process typically is conducted as a centrally orchestrated exercise (Bower, 1970; Bower and Gilbert, 2005). As a consequence, only the largest investment decisions are typically made by top management whereas many important decisions are taken by managers responsible for locally dispersed operations. Hence, a more complete understanding of the multinational strategy-making process should comprise a mixture of formal planning activities conducted at the corporate headquarters and more or less autonomous initiatives taken in the various parts of the organization, including the overseas business entities.

The middle managers operating across the multinational organization are arguably instrumental in the process to foster autonomous local initiatives with the aim of accomplishing the long-term strategic goals of the corporation. In this context Nonaka (1988) refers to a *deductive* top-down and an *inductive* bottom-up strategy process where the aspirations expressed by top management can interact fruitfully with initiatives taken by lower-level operators with middle managers acting as important liaisons between the top and bottom. Such a process will rely on decisions made by managers operating deep inside the organization with open communication to discuss emerging business opportunities and coordinate initiatives to exploit those possibilities in a changing environment. This reflects an *evolutionary* strategy-making perspective (e.g., Burgelman, 1996) where lower-level managers are the instigators of new business initiatives, whereas the role of top management is to structure an organization with policies to guide and enable autonomous managerial engagements throughout the corporation.

Hence, it is shown that the ability to deploy alternative strategy-making modes under different competitive conditions and combine, e.g., central command and autonomous approaches, will create flexibility associated with superior performance outcomes (Hart, 1992; Hart and Banbury, 1994). Other studies find supportive evidence that firms with an ability to combine rational analytical planning activities with autonomous responsive actions enabled by a decentralized decision structure will outperform their close competitors in the industries (e.g., Andersen, 2004; Baum and Wally, 2003). Hence, multinational organizations that are able to respond to ongoing changes in the turbulent global markets and adapt business activities to better match the changing market requirements will consistently achieve higher average returns compared to peers in their industry with a lower variability (risk) in performance outcomes (e.g., Andersen et al., 2007; Andersen and Bettis, 2015). In short, the ability to adapt the multinational business activities effectively to turbulent changes under global competitive conditions requires a certain balance between strategies induced by top management at headquarters and autonomous initiatives taken by local managers operating throughout the organization.

International business

Over the past decades where the theoretical foundations for contemporary strategy-making practices have evolved, the competitive environment has changed dramatically due to ongoing globalization efforts as well as fundamental technological advancements. We have witnessed sustained efforts to extend international commerce and capital flows deregulating national barriers to trade and foreign investments, e.g., under the umbrella of the World Trade Organization (WTO). Various regional free-trade zones and political collaborative arrangements have emerged including, e.g., the European Union (EU), the North American Free Trade Agreement (NAFTA), the Andean Community in South America, and the Association of Southeast Asian Nations (ASEAN). So, while some talk about a continuous move towards globalization of business activities, others refer to increasing business interactions within major regional market spheres that in turn interact with each other (e.g., Rugman, 1981). Recently, the European Union (EU) was affected by the UK referendum deciding to leave the political union. This so-called *Brexit* was partially a result of a majority of the British people feeling unhappy about the increasing centralization of power within the EU. Some see Brexit as symptomatic of a recent international phenomenon: a populist backlash in western politics against globalization (Rachman, 2016). Yet, others see it as a way for the UK to become even more free, globalized and open-minded as the country will be less dependent on a regional centralized power. Disregarding these few events within the regional free-trade zones there has been a general move towards more open trade and investment relationships throughout the world over the past decades. New advanced telecommunication capabilities and the global reach of the Internet have enabled entirely new possibilities for multinational strategic organization. It has allowed more instantaneous interaction between corporate business entities located in different parts of the world enabling more integrated globally dispersed production and distribution facilities. The implied global communication capabilities have provided unprecedented ways of exchanging operating data, market insights and knowledge more effectively across networks of individuals than has ever been possible. Since capital flows primarily are executed in the form of electronic bits exchanged between accounts located in different national jurisdictions, the improved information technology has supported global capital transfer and investment activities. At the same time the transportation technologies and logistics systems supporting the exchange of physical goods around the globe have advanced considerably with constant increases in cost efficiencies and streamlining of international transportation networks linking important trading partners together.

This development has opened up for new multinational business opportunities and has also changed the strategic consideration towards a more globally competitive view where threats and opportunities are represented across a much broader scope of international markets than has been the case before. The increased access to overseas markets combined with possibilities for international travels both for private and business purposes has formed a basis for a certain cultural integration or has at least increased the exposure between different national cultures with direct exchanges between individuals going in and out between different social networks in different cultural contexts. For some constituents and for certain types of products and services this has formed areas of common tastes thereby creating a basis for developing global offerings with broader appeal in different parts of the world. While this may not apply to all types of goods and services, it has changed the way we typically consider global market opportunities where commercial success somehow implies eventual scalability of business activities to comprise all the major markets and regions around the world.

The changing environmental context has added new aspects to the strategic management considerations of firms that operate internationally. That is, the expanded possibilities for conducting business on a global scale with operations located in different national market environments adds a number of specific concerns to the general strategic considerations. What makes an international business perspective special in this context is the fact that multinational organizations operate across more national boundaries, which adds more complexity to the equation. There may be smaller or larger cultural differences between different national markets and geographical regions reflected in different linguistic barriers and differences in social values, behavioral norms, customs and tastes. This may also be reflected in different business practices, economic infrastructures and institutional settings for business conduct. The greater the exposure to more of these potential culturally bounded differences, the more will be accumulated into a concern for *liabilities of foreignness* (Zaheer, 1996; Zaheer and Musakowski, 1997). That is, the more diverse the national contexts in which the multinational organization operates, the more energy and managerial focus must be devoted to deal with overseas operations governed in vastly different ways from the home country.

In other words, the changing context for global business activities represents both a promising value potential deriving from new business opportunities as well as threats from more intense international competition and challenges in dealing with diverse business conditions across geographical regions. The opportunities associated with an extended multinational reach include the potential for sales growth, scale and scope economies, cross-border arbitrage, lower factor costs and the innovative potential associated with diverse resources and business activities across more markets. The downside concerns of multinationality include increasing costs of coordinating diverse business activities, processing more information, and managing liabilities of foreignness, all of which tend to increase with the geographical reach of the multinational organization. In addition to this, a global presence with investment in productive assets may increase exposure to potential economic crises, political and social conflicts, and other risk factors including natural disasters, fraudulent behaviors, security issues, etc. that may be overlooked in the home country because it is of little concern in familiar surroundings.

Multinational strategy-making

The international business literature has considered how firm-specific advantages may drive a multinational organization to engage in foreign direct investment expanding the international business activities of the corporation (e.g., Dunning, 1979; Vernon, 1971). From a headquarter perspective the local subsidiaries are seen as vehicles transmitting unique corporate capabilities with a capacity to achieve superior performance into overseas markets without any need for modification to cater to the local markets. In later extensions, the tension between concerns for global efficiency pressures and local adaptation to national market needs was seen as a central strategic theme in the multinational organization (Prahalad and Doz, 1987). This introduced a preoccupation with the specific structure applied to manage the multinational business activities as exemplified by typologies represented by global, international, multi-domestic (multinational) or transnational strategies (Bartlett and Ghoshal, 1989). This thinking promoted the existence of a proper balance between the dual pressures for global integration to gain economic efficiency and local responsiveness to satisfy specific needs in national markets with an overarching aim of achieving both efficiency and effectiveness at the same time.

Given the high turbulence of global market environments, this may be achievable if the local business unit managers are allowed to use their own local contacts and alliances to deal with emerging issues rather than relying on a general central approach imposed by the corporate headquarters (Doz et al., 1981). This opens up the possibility that competitive advantage in the multination organization is achieved in a global structure that combines an ability to adapt local market offerings to local needs through informal coordination carried out in self-established networks of internal and external collaborators, bound together by effective communication links.

Hence, the multinational organizations that operate in dynamic and complex global contexts can use effective information-processing capabilities to coordinate interdependent responsive tasks across different business units as well as monitor and communicate information about environmental changes (e.g., Galbraith, 1977, 1994). The increasing amounts of information to be handled in these organizations impose high demands on the intra-organizational information and communication exchange systems (Egelhoff, 1982; Tushman and Nadler, 1978). The *vertical* communication

BOX 2.1 The strategy-making typologies in international business

The establishment of strategy typologies within the context of dual pressures for global economic efficiency and differentiation towards local market conditions has served to pinpoint particular strategy exemplars to illustrate how firms may choose to structure and operate their multinational strategy-making process with respect to these two dimensions. As is often the case, no firm may fit squarely into any of these rather idealized typologies. They are mainly established for pedagogical reasons to clarify an underlying logic developed through the study of concrete business cases. While the extant research literature for a while tried to study the prevalence and effectiveness of the stylized typologies in their proposed environmental settings, the results have been rather unequivocal. The fact of the matter is that in turbulent global market environments the underlying competitive landscape is under constant change and may therefore gradually change prior conventional wisdom as well as complicate longitudinal quantitative studies trying to identify optimal strategy-making modes.

Two other aspects seem worthy of consideration. The first is that the structural complexity of contemporary multinational organizations can mean that different parts of the same corporation may simultaneously emphasize different strategic orientations. The second is that both dimensions of global efficiency pressures and local responsiveness pressures are not bifocal constructs of high and low but constitute continuous variables with a multiplicity of possible combinations. Hence, even though Matsushita is often characterized as pursuing a global strategy, L. M. Ericsson an international strategy, and Unilever a multinational strategy, they all try to combine elements of all the typologies across different parts of the corporate structure (Figure 2.1).

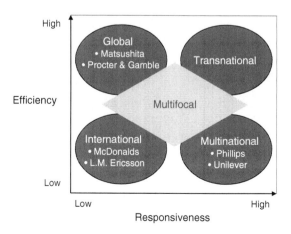

FIGURE 2.1 Multifocal aspects of the multinational strategy-making typologies.

The contemporary Unilever organization is often described a transnational company that evolved by responding to the local market needs where they had a presence, that is, being global and acting locally. The company has proximity to local markets and can respond to local changes while securing economies of scale from a global operating structure where information is exchanged across all units of the global organization.

Furthermore, the implication of the two continuous dimensions is that, to some extent, they represent a trade-off between economic efficiencies achieved through integrated standardization and differentiation flexibilities achieved through local responsiveness (Figure 2.2). However, it is entirely possible to combine the two concerns along a type of efficiency-flexibility frontier through conscious design efforts.

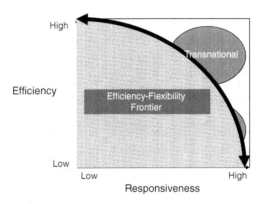

FIGURE 2.2 The efficiency-flexibility trade-off in the integration-responsiveness framework.

flows up and down the hierarchical management levels typically relate to formal control systems where structured information is reported for regular monitoring purposes. The *horizontal* communication flows typically comprise more unstructured information that is exchanged laterally between managers in different business units and geographical locations (Tushman and Nadler, 1978).

Multinational organizations must be able to coordinate intangible resources and specialized process knowledge when dealing with dynamic and complex interdependencies across the global business activities and respond effectively to the changing conditions across different markets (Child and McGrath, 2001). Local responsiveness is easier to handle when decision-making power is moved closer to the business units that have the relevant market information available and local knowledge to deal with unexpected emerging developments. IT-enhanced communication and information systems can help managers distribute information where relevant data are available across all the local decision nodes (Brynjolfsson and Mendelson, 1993). These communication networks can support the informal exchange of unstructured tacit knowledge, insights, and experiences in open discussions about emerging conditions and the coordination of responsive actions.

International business research adopted the integration-responsiveness (I-R) framework (Figure 2.3) to better understand how to organize an extended international presence and the two dimensions identified the typological choices between the two strategic orientations (Prahalad and Doz, 1987; Harzing, 2000). Research on the I-R framework has focused on how different industry characteristics determined by external market conditions has induced firms to engage in cross-border business activities to manage their international business expansion. The resource-based view (RBV) has also been adopted to explain the sourcing aspects of multinational enterprise (e.g., Tallman and Li, 1996). This perspective sees successful internationalization as building on unique multinational resource bundles that can drive sustainable competitive advantage as unique organizational capabilities operationalize the pressures for global efficiency and local responsiveness (Venaik et al., 2004). Hence, the combined focus on market- and resource-based perspectives can provide a better understanding about the pursuit of alternative international business strategies.

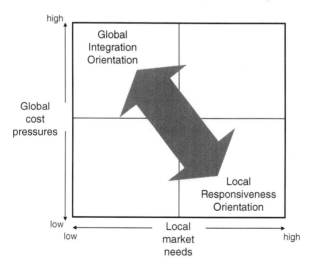

FIGURE 2.3   The strategic orientations towards global integration and local responsiveness.

The consideration for differentiation and integration was initially introduced in analyses of organizational structure (Lawrence and Lorsch, 1967) and later adopted in multinational management studies (Prahalad and Doz, 1987; Bartlett and Ghoshal, 1989). Differentiation was defined as *segmentation* of organizational subsystems specialized to deal with particular environmental requirements and *integration* was seen as a process of uniting the subsystems to fulfill the organizational purpose. The distinction between differentiation and integration was used to argue how multinational organizations must respond to local market needs through differentiated activities while the diverse activities should be integrated to achieve economic efficiency (Prahalad and Doz, 1987). Market pressures to hone specific requirements in each of the national environmental contexts would drive a need for local responsiveness, whereas global cost pressures would drive a need for economic efficiency through operational integration and coordination to obtain economies of scale and scope.

The two dimensions of local responsiveness and global integration identified the four generic global, multidomestic (multinational), international and transnational strategies (Bartlett and Ghoshal, 1989). Global integration is typically associated with relatively homogeneous products in industries like electronic equipment, consumer electronics, computer products, mobile phones, etc. (Prahalad and Doz, 1987; Bartlett and Ghoshal, 1989). In other industries the market characteristics may differ substantially across national borders creating pressure for local responsiveness, say in household goods industries like food, clothing, furniture, etc. (Prahalad and Doz, 1987; Beamish et al., 1997).

An orientation towards *global integration* implies that operational management is centralized where resource-committing decisions are coordinated in a central planning function in line with the overarching corporate strategy (Prahalad and Doz, 1987). It constitutes a centralized structural configuration where complex interdependencies are coordinated at the corporate level. Decision-making is carried out in accordance with the central planning process and scaled globally where the local business entities pursue activities in accordance with the strategies mandated by headquarters (Bartlett and Ghoshal, 1989; Harzing, 2000). An orientation towards *local responsiveness* implies an ability of local business entities to accommodate national market conditions by taking responsive action in a decentralized decision structure (Prahalad and Doz, 1987). So, authority and decision-making power is delegated to managers who have local and regional market responsibilities, with freedom to generate resources in the local market. It constitutes a loosely coupled organizational structure with distributed decision-making capabilities (Bartlett and Ghoshal, 1989, 1999; Harzing, 2000).

The international business literature has examined the validity of the proposed strategy typologies determined within the I-R framework (e.g., Roth and Morrison, 1990, Harzing, 2000). Some studies found broad support for the strategy typologies (Roth and Morrison, 1990) whereas others were unable to identify distinct strategy clusters among firms in the electronics, computers and chemical industries (Leong and Tan, 1993). Whereas subsequent studies have found some conformity to the typologies (e.g., Harzing, 2000) the verdict is far from a final resolution. The underlying reasoning implicitly assumes that the strategy typologies applied within their proper market contexts will be associated with superior performance outcomes. However, this implication of the I-R framework has barely been studied across different industrial environments.

It was suggested that the structural characteristics of industries including scale economies, national comparative advantages and converging customer demands would determine the multinational organizations' propensities towards global integration and local responsiveness orientations (e.g., Birkinshaw et al., 1995). This kind of reasoning would suggest that industries, such as those involving food products, consumer goods and metal fabrication, would tend to adopt a local responsiveness orientation where industries, such as, semiconductors, computers and automobiles would tend to assume a global integration orientation. Industries with global standards like computer products and consumer electronics are presumed to face high global cost pressures thus adopting a global integration orientation in pursuit of a *global strategy* (Figure 2.4). In contrast, food processing, clothing, and other household goods industries operating under pressure of specific national market conditions should assume a local responsiveness orientation in pursuit of a *multidomestic strategy* (Beamish et al., 1997).

Higher technology intensity seems to push multinational organizations towards global integration and is typically found in communication equipment, electronic components, semiconductors and computer industries. So, firms operating in computer products industries are often presumed to pursue a global strategy. In industries with rather standardized global products the need for efficiency is substantial and is expected to derive from operational integration and resource coordination through the central planning process at corporate headquarters (Prahalad and Doz, 1987; Bartlett and Ghoshal, 1989). To the extent computer products become commoditized, the global cost pressures should increase and push towards a global integration orientation. On the other hand, heterogeneous resources availability from across a multinational organization provides a basis for developing firm-specific competencies that can lead to new business opportunities. Diverse insights and experiences from different market environments give access to unique resource bundles across the multinational organization that can favor dynamic technology-driven industries. These potential global sourcing advantages may not only apply to physical input factors but also to knowledge-based resources that can

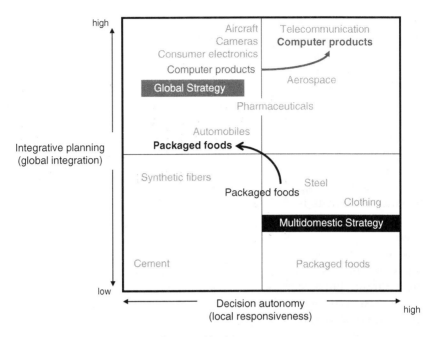

FIGURE 2.4 Strategic orientations and industry context.

support the creation of new business opportunities in technology-intense industries (e.g., Bartlett and Ghoshal, 1989; Andersen and Foss, 2005). Turbulent global business environments require a certain degree of decision autonomy to foster innovation from diverse knowledge available across diverse international markets (e.g., Foss and Pedersen, 2002). As a consequence, firms in dynamic knowledge-based industries may continue to pursue global integration while also increasingly emphasizing local responsiveness to exploit technological know-how from product adaptations and technology developments in local markets. So, firms in technology-intense businesses, like computer products, may increasingly adopt a strategic orientation of global integration combined with local responsiveness to gain competitive advantage (Figure 2.4).

It has been argued that common household goods like food, clothing and furniture for basic consumption are more influenced by local traditions, habits and tastes embedded in national or regional cultures (Beamish et al., 1997). In accordance with this logic it is suggested that a local responsiveness orientation is more appropriate for multinational organizations with business activities in food processing and clothing industries (Prahalad and Doz, 1987). However, while many firms in the household and common goods industries operate in diverse national markets with deeply ingrained cultures there is also a general trend towards developing strong global brands in these industries that appeal to a broader, less differentiated, globally oriented audience. For these reasons many of those firms may increasingly try to standardize their global products with a focus on highly recognizable brands. For this reason there may be an increasing emphasis on standardization and integration to gain efficiency around the promotion of global brands as they are distributed across a larger global market (e.g., Sciulli and Taiani, 2001). Therefore, firms operating in common goods businesses, such as food processing, that pursue internationalization across multinational markets may increasingly adopt a strategic orientation of global integration (Figure 2.4).

The choice between strategic orientations in dynamic and complex international markets is in constant flux because of changing competitive pressures and technological innovations that affect the strategy recommendations derived from analyses of yesteryears' business contexts. Hence, we observe a move from a global strategy focus towards a transnational strategy in turbulent computer products industries, to better access and utilize the innovative potential of knowledge-based resources in local markets. We also see a move from a predominant multidomestic strategy of local responsiveness in less dynamic common goods industries orientation towards a focus on global strategy and a global integration orientation to accommodate branded products. So, while firms in less dynamic industries may see an increased need for global efficiency, firms in technology-intense hypercompetitive markets may also increasingly depend on gaining access to local knowledge-based competencies for ongoing innovation.

Multinational corporate strategy

The international business and strategic management literatures share some common elements, although they have evolved fairly separately as two distinct research streams in two relatively distinct academic fields. The study of international business strategy is dominated by the dual concerns for global efficiency and local responsiveness. In this context, the conventional strategy view is that of a rational analytical planning process prepared for subsequent implementation by the multinational organization where outcomes are monitored regularly by top management at the corporate center. To this is added the insight that a great many resource-committing decisions are made by local managers scattered throughout the organization and these emergent autonomous initiatives can turn into path-breaking strategic opportunities that may fundamentally influence the future strategic direction of the corporation. Hence, effective multinational strategy-making processes must somehow simultaneously take coordination obtained through central strategic planning as well as the decentralized local entrepreneurial responses into account. Voilà! Here we see pretty comparable pressures between integration/coordination and autonomy/responsiveness play out in the two fields of study. So, there are common traits in the way both the fields of strategic management and international business conceive the strategy-making challenges.

Most contemporary firms operate business activities in more than one national market and offer several more or less related products and services in these markets. Some firms may be more selective in their choice of geographical presence with a focus on specific national market contexts where other firms may operate in multiple countries around the globe. However, the vast majority of firms manage more than one product, offering across several countries at the same time, which means that we effectively can apply the term *multinational corporation* to these predominant firms that operate multiple business activities across multiple national contexts (Ghemawat, 2002). The considerations for the optimal composition and management of a business portfolio are normally referred to as a *corporate strategy* as opposed to a business strategy, which is concerned with the strategy of a single product-market. This is contrasted with a *multinational strategy*, which can be said to be concerned with the composition and optimal choice of presence across national markets. However, the considerations made within these two strategy areas share many comparable economic trade-offs.

A number of positive arguments support the considerations for an extended corporate business portfolio. Hence, increasing organizational size may provide more *bargaining power*, creating economic muscle in business negotiations. This makes it possible to extend existing administrative functions to cover a broader set of activities that can *save cost*. Similarly, corporate resources can be pooled to accomplish common ends across multiple businesses that release *economic efficiencies*. At the same time, increased diversity of business practices may enhance the ability to *innovate* and create new valuable products and services. Increased business volume across a portfolio of related business activities can provide a basis for *scale economies* with standardized operations and *scope economies* sharing related processes across businesses. These positive effects from a larger portfolio of businesses may well display *diminishing return* characteristics with lower incremental benefits from marginal increases in business activities. However, there may also be potential negative effects associated with an extended business portfolio. The management of disparate businesses requires considerable effort to coordinate activities that impose additional costs, particularly the more unrelated the business activities and the more turbulent the particular industries are. At the same time essential strategic resources may be *overstretched* when trying to apply them across multiple business activities at the same time. The diminishing returns from positive effects and the increasing negative cost effects generally suggest an inverse curvilinear relationship between business diversification and corporate performance.

We find comparable rationales applied to the consideration of the geographical expansion of corporate business activities. A common internationalization perspective describes the proper process as a gradual expansion of business activities, first in the markets located close by that most resemble the home market and then gradually extended to more distant regions as corporate activities grow (e.g., Johanson and Vahlne, 1977). An extended geographical reach of large corporations may reflect a particular *multinationality advantage* ascribed to a global firm engaged in foreign direct investments. This opens up fundamental questions about the economic rationales that can explain the trend towards larger multinational organizations. Here, a number of factors seek to argue for the value derived from a broader multinational presence and many of the arguments resemble those applied to business diversification. These include the potential for gaining economic efficiency across multinational markets and developing new business opportunities from access to diverse resources and capabilities across diverse markets. The arguments for potential scale and scope economies also apply to geographical expansion where a higher degree of *multinationality* reflects increased business activities across more national markets. This provides opportunities for more cost efficient standardized production facilities at central locations shared across a larger number of local markets and may enable the sharing of capabilities across compatible markets (Buckley and Casson, 1976; Kobrin, 1991). The ability to access more diverse business environments can inspire the development of business opportunities and foster *innovation* for new products and services (Bartlett and Ghoshal, 1999; Govindarajan and Gupta, 2001). The broader multinational factor endowments will provide opportunities for more effective orchestration of corporate activities, giving access to more cost-effective factor inputs with *arbitrage* opportunities between national markets (Rugman, 1981; Teece, 1981). Furthermore, a multinational structure of business activities creates potential *flexibilities* where the productive capacities can be switched between foreign entities to take advantage of changes in economic conditions (Kogut, 1985; Kogut and Kulatilaka, 1994).

We can also account for potential negative effects from multinational expansion where a major negative effect relates to the increasing *coordination costs* associated with the management of an extended geographic presence across multiple and diverse national market contexts. This might show an exponential increase in costs as the degree of multinationality increases (Jones and Hill, 1988; Roth and O'Donnell, 1996) because increasingly diverse environments result in more handling and greater coordination of business transactions between potentially disparate market contexts. Foreign operations in more distant geographical locations can also lead to significant increases in communication costs, travel expenses, legal fees, etc. It is not inconceivable that it will require significantly more managerial involvement and executive attention that will increase costs and draw on scarce and expensive leadership resources. Finally, the managerial demands imposed by the particular distinctiveness of national market characteristics put additional requirements on management typically referred to as *liabilities of foreignness* (Zaheer, 1996; Zaheer and Musakowski, 1997). The coordination costs and costs derived from liabilities of foreignness cannot be extracted directly from the accounting ledgers or reported accounts, but are typically hidden as overtime pay, travel expenses, etc. The implied diversity of national business operations and human interactions across disparate cultures may impose exponentially increasing costs if the associated management challenges escalate. But, it is also possible that an organization can learn to deal with the cultural differences so the associated costs can be contained.

The aggregated effects on performance derived from the positive and negative factors can be assessed for different degrees of multinationality, indicated as the number of international markets where the corporation has a presence. The proposed advantages might show linear or curvilinear relationships to the degree of multinationality, and aggregating these effects can provide insights about the potential net advantages from extended multinational business activities (Figure 2.5).

Under idealized conditions, the net effect of multinational expansion shows an inverse u-shaped relationship to corporate performance as the degree of multinationality increases. However, the final verdict is less than equivocal at this point, where a rich empirical literature suggests many

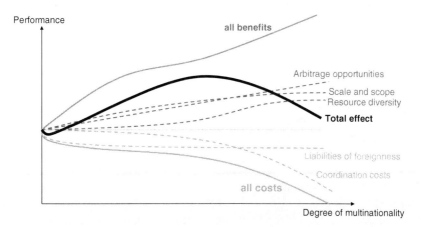

FIGURE 2.5 The positive and negative effects associated with multinational activities.

different alternative performance effects. Yet, this particular performance pattern of multinational expansion is found to apply to knowledge-intensive industry context and only to a lesser extent in other capital-intensive industries (Andersen, 2012). That is, multinational expansion, or geographical diversification as it is, may display a performance pattern comparable to that observed in the case of corporate business diversification. From this vantage point, we can think of a potentially optimal point, for the *multinational corporation*, that considers the best possible combination of both business and geographical diversification (Figure 2.6). This is obtained, for a degree of business diversification, somewhere between dominant and unrelated business activities and in a multinational structure adapted to the firm-specific conditions with some overseas presence, but not excessively so.

The performance outcomes related to the degree of multinationality is dependent on the industry context in which the firm operates (Andersen, 2008, 2012). The potential for responsive flexibility associated with a diverse geographical presence is particularly pronounced in information-driven knowledge-intensive industries[1] and lead to an inverse u-shaped curvilinear relationship to corporate performance (Figure 2.6). The reason for this net effect is that knowledge-intense information in these business activities can be stored electronically in computers and in the heads of key people that conduct the business activities. This form of information and knowledge is rather flexible and easy to move between geographical locations, as the exchange of electronic information and people carries a relatively low cost. These particular features make it fairly easy to recombine knowledge and, with little cost, link it to new

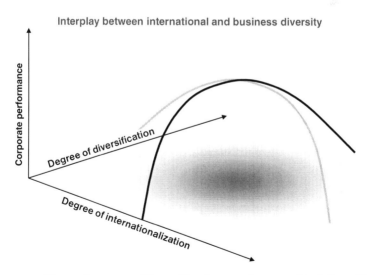

Interplay between international and business diversity

FIGURE 2.6   The performance effects of business and geographical diversification.

innovative initiatives and development of cross-border business opportunities. This particular context appeals to flexible and nimble maneuvering where multinational business activities can be more easily modified, restructured and adapted towards activities that create a better fit with current market conditions.

Summary

Combining central forward-looking planning processes at corporate headquarters with autonomous responses at local business entities provides the means to deal with a turbulent global business environment and satisfies the dual requests for global integration and local responsiveness (I-R). The prescriptive I-R framework is dynamic and conventional strategy recommendations change as the competitive conditions evolve in the turbulent global markets. The multinational corporation is faced with comparable considerations for business and geographic diversification where the optimum can provide higher returns with a favorable risk profile.

Note

1 These industries comprise business activities such as information services, accounting, auditing, consulting, engineering and management advisory services.

References

Andersen, T. J. (2004). Integrating decentralized strategy making and strategic planning processes in dynamic environments. *Journal of Management Studies*, **41**(8): 1271–1299.
Andersen, T. J. (2008). Multinational performance relationships and industry context, SMG Working Paper 15/2008, Copenhagen Business School.
Andersen, T. J. (2012). Multinational risk and performance outcomes: Effects of knowledge intensity and industry context. *International Business Review*, **21**: 239–252.
Andersen, T. J. and Bettis, R. A. (2015). Exploring longitudinal risk-return relationships. *Strategic Management Journal*, **36**(8): 1135–1145.
Andersen, T. J. and Foss, N. J. (2005). Strategic opportunity and economic performance in multinational enterprises: The role and effects of information and communication technology. *Journal of International Management*, **11**(2): 293–310.
Andersen, T. J., Denrell, J. and Bettis, R. A. (2007). Strategic responsiveness and Bowman's risk-return paradox, *Strategic Management Journal*, **28**: 407–429.
Anthony, R. N. (1965). *Planning and Control Systems: A Framework for Analysis*. Division of Research, Graduate School of Business Administration, Harvard University.
Bartlett, C. and Ghoshal, S. (1989). *The Transnational Corporation*. New York, NY: The Free Press.

Bartlett, C. A. and Ghoshal, S. (1999). *Managing Across Borders: The Transnational Solution* (vol. 2). Boston, MA: Harvard Business School Press.

Baum, J. and Wally, S. (2003). Strategic decision speed and firm performance. *Strategic Management Journal*, **24**(11): 1107–1129.

Beamish, P. W., Morrison, A. J. and Rosenzweig, P. M. (1997). *International Management: Text and Cases*. Boston, MA: Irwin, McGraw-Hill.

Birkinshaw, J., Morrison, A. and Hulland, J. (1995). Structural and competitive determinants of a global integration strategy. *Strategic Management Journal*, **16**(8): 637–655.

Bower, J. L. (1970). Managing the resource allocation process: A study of corporate planning and investment. Boston, MA: Harvard Business School.

Bower, J. L. and Gilbert, C. G. (2005). *From Resource Allocation to Strategy*. Oxford, UK: Oxford University Press.

Brynjolfsson, E. and Mendelson, H. (1993). Information systems and the organization of modern enterprise. *Journal of Organizational Computing and Electronic Commerce*, **3**(3): 245–255.

Buckley, P. J. and Casson, M. C. (1976). *The Future of the Multinational Enterprise*. London, UK: Macmillan.

Burgelman, R. A. (1983). Corporate entrepreneurship and strategic management: Insights from a process study. *Management Science*, **29**(12): 1349–1364.

Burgelman, R. A. (1996). A process model of strategic business exit: Implications for an evolutionary perspective on strategy. *Strategic Management Journal*, **17**(S1): 193–214.

Burgelman, R. A. and Grove, A. S. (1996). Strategic dissonance. *California Management Review*, **38**(2): 8–28.

Child, J. and McGrath, R. G. (2001). Organizations unfettered: Organizational form in an information-intensive economy. *Academy of Management Journal*, **44**(6): 1135–1148.

Doz, Y. L., Bartlett, C. A. and Prahalad, C. K. (1981). Global competitive pressures and host country demands: Managing tensions in MNCs. *California Management Review*, **23**(3): 63–74.

Dunning, J. H. (1980). Toward an eclectic theory of international production: Some empirical tests. *Journal of International Business Studies*, **11**(1): 9–31.

Egelhoff, W. G. (1982). Strategy and structure in multinational corporations: An information-processing approach. *Administrative Science Quarterly*, 435–458.

Foss, N. J. and Pedersen, T. (2002). Transferring knowledge in MNCs: The role of sources of subsidiary knowledge and organizational context. *Journal of International Management*, **8**(1): 49–67.

Galbraith, J. R. (1977). *Organization Design*. Reading, MA: Addison-Wesley Publishing Company.

Galbraith, J. R. (1994). *Competing with Flexible Lateral Organizations*. Reading, MA: Addison-Wesley.

Ghemawat, P. (2002). Semiglobalization and international business strategy. *Journal of International Business Studies*, **34**(2): 138–152.

Govindarajan, V. and Gupta, A. K. (2001). *The Quest for Global Dominance: Transforming Global Presence into Global Competitive Advantage*. San Francisco, CA: Jossey-Bass.

Hart, S. and Banbury, C. (1994). How strategy-making processes can make a difference. *Strategic Management Journal*, **15**(4): 251–269.

Hart, S. L. (1992). An integrative framework for strategy-making processes. *Academy of Management Review*, **17**(2): 327–351.

Harzing, A. W. (2000). An empirical analysis and extension of the Bartlett and Ghoshal typology of multinational companies. *Journal of International Business Studies*, **31**(1): 101–120.

Johanson, J. and Vahlne, J. E. (1977). The internationalization process of the firm: A model of knowledge development and increasing foreign commitments. *Journal of International Business Studies*, **8**(1): 23–32.

Jones, G. R. and Hill, C. W. L. (1988). Transaction cost analysis of strategy-structure choice. *Strategic Management Journal*, **9**: 159–172.

Kobrin, S. J. (1991). An empirical analysis of the determinants of global integration. *Strategic Management Journal*, **12**: 17–37.

Kogut, B. (1985). Designing global strategies: Profiting from operational flexibility. *Sloan Management Review*, Fall: 27–38.

Kogut, B. and Kulatilaka, N. (1994). Operating flexibility, global manufacturing and the open value of a multinational network. *Management Science*, **40**: 123–138.

Lawrence, P. R. and Lorsch, J. W. (1967). Differentiation and integration in complex organizations. *Administrative Science Quarterly*, 1–47.

Leong, S. M. and Tan, C. T. (1993). Managing across borders: An empirical test of the Bartlett and Ghoshal [1989] organizational typology. *Journal of International Business Studies*, **24**(3): 449–464.

Noda, T. and Bower, J. L. (1996). Strategy making as iterated processes of resource allocation. *Strategic Management Journal*, **17**(S1): 159–192.

Nonaka, I. (1988). Toward middle-up-down management: accelerating information creation. *Sloan Management Review*, **29**(3): 9–18.

Prahalad, C. K. and Doz, Y. L. (1987). *The Multinational Mission*. New York, NY: The Free Press.

Rachman, G. (2016). Brexit and the making of a global crisis. *Financial Times*, June 24. Retrieved on June 24, 2016 from http://www.ft.com/cms/s/0/5490d754-3a0e-11e6-9a05-82a9b15a8ee7.html?siteedition=intl#axzz4H6upYMCo.

Roth, K. and Morrison, A. J. (1990). An empirical analysis of the integration-responsiveness framework in global industries. *Journal of International Business Studies*, **21**(4): 541–564.

Roth, K. and O'Donnell, S. (1996). Foreign subsidiary compensation strategy: An agency theory perspective. *Academy of Management Journal*, **39**: 678–703.

Rugman, A. M. (1981). *Inside the Multinational: The Economics of International Markets*. London, UK: Croom Helm.

Schendel, D. and Hofer, C. W. (eds.) (1979). *Strategic Management: A New View of Business Policy and Planning*. Boston, MA: Little, Brown.

Sciulli, L. M. and Taiani, V. (2001). Advertising content for the global audience: A research proposal. *Competitiveness Review: An International Business Journal*, **11**(2): 39–47.

Tallman, S. and Li, J. (1996). Effects of international diversity and product diversity on the performance of multinational firms. *Academy of Management Journal*, **39**(1): 179–196.

Teece, D. J. (1981). The multinational enterprise: Market failure and market power considerations. *Sloan Management Review*, Spring: 3–17.

Tushman, M. L. and Nadler, D. A. (1978). Information processing as an integrating concept in organizational design. *Academy of Management Review*, **3**(3): 613–624.

Venaik, S., Midgley, D. F. and Devinney, T. M. (2004). A new perspective on the integration-responsiveness pressures confronting multinational firms. *Management International Review* (15–48). Wiesbaden, Germany: Gabler Verlag.

Vernon, R. (1971). Sovereignty at bay: The multinational spread of US enterprises. *The International Executive*, **13**(4): 1–3.

Zaheer, S. (1996). Overcoming the liabilities of foreignness. *Academy of Management Journal*, **38**: 341–363.

Zaheer, S. and Musakowski, E. (1997). The dynamics of the liability of foreignness: A global study of survival in financial services. *Strategic Management Journal*, **18**: 439–464.

3

ORGANIZING TO DEAL WITH A DYNAMIC GLOBAL CONTEXT

Key points

- Technology innovation and creative destruction
- Forming an effective multinational organizational structure
- Distributed networks for collaborative learning
- Interaction between center and periphery

The global business context is characterized by uncertainty and turbulence affected by technology-driven changes in information-processing and communication capabilities. These forces affect the way multinational organizations can operate under frequent changes and increasingly complex conditions. In this environmental context it becomes important to manage the implied strategic exposures in ways that can exploit emerging opportunities arising from the changing context while building a resilient corporate structure of multinational business operations.

The multinational strategic reasoning is influenced by two major theoretical frameworks grounded in industrial economics (e.g., Chen, 1996; Porter, 1980, 2008) and a resource-based view of the firm (e.g., Barney, 1986, 1991; Porter, 1985; Teece, 2007). The industrial economic logic suggests that the firm should take advantage of potential strengths in bargaining positions towards other economic agents so as to improve its competitive position vis-à-vis potential rivals in multiple markets around the world. At best this will provide economic benefits in commercial transactions and contractual negotiations that form a basis for extracting higher returns from the underlying business activities. The resource-based view argues that the uniqueness of valuable capabilities and productive assets (or resources broadly defined) underpins the ability to generate higher returns either caused by superior operational efficiencies or because internal processes lead to more effective outcomes (Barney, 1986; 1991; Wernerfelt, 1984). Sustainable competitive advantage (SCA), defined as the ability to maintain excess returns over extended periods of time, is thus dependent on the stickiness and inimitable characteristics of the underlying resources that generate those excess returns. This constitutes a type of interim equilibrium where other competing firms are unable to erode this advantage by duplication, imitation or other mimicking behavior. However, under hypercompetitive conditions potentially advantageous resource positions are constantly challenged by ongoing innovative efforts to develop competing offerings that sooner or later will make current products and services obsolete. The implied reduction in the sustainability of competitive advantage fostered the idea of *dynamic capabilities* presenting the notion that firms must be able to recombine available resources in new, more effective constellations on an ongoing basis, in order to adapt to observed changes in the competitive environment (Teece et al., 1997; Teece, 2007, 2010).

The study of innovation and its economic effects is an almost classical field, often associated with Schumpeter's concept of *creative destruction* as a pillar for economic development and growth in open economies. As others have before him and since, Schumpeter (1939) studied the contours of business cycles and reasoned that the ability to generate periods of high economic growth had to stem from innovation, that is, the human capacity to generate entirely new technologies serving as engines for exceptional increases in productivity. In other words, there seemed to be time periods or *waves* of exceptional growth imposed by the introduction of new technologies that disrupt and outcompete prior technologies. That is, the dynamics of an open economic system constantly fosters innovation and is therefore also a source of cyclical instability and economic shocks. These *Schumpeterian shocks* may lead to significant changes in the global business environment. Schumpeter (1942) saw entrepreneurial behavior as an economic dynamo that runs everything, where individual entrepreneurs across firms of all sizes and ages are agents of the innovation that leads to *creative destruction*. It is the innovative projects of these entrepreneurs that generate jobs, income and economic progress for society.

It has been observed that increasing economic growth rates typically take off when new technology innovations, adopted for general economic use, are fronted by the emergence of *lead industries* (Thompson, 1990). In the past, three such waves of accelerating growth have been noted and described. From the 1780s onwards, the first wave included industries that evolved around water power, cotton textiles and iron, until the middle of the nineteenth century where subsequent lead industries, in a second wave, focused on steam power, railways, and steel production that dominated until the latter part of that century (Figure 3.1). This was followed by a third wave around new technology-driven industries based on the combustion engine, motor vehicles, electric energy and chemicals for a period until the mid-nineteen hundreds towards a fourth wave driven by electronics, semiconductors and aerospace technologies from the mid-nineteen hundreds. The current and fifth wave, which took off from the 1990s, has been dominated by computer-based technologies, digitization, Internet usage and mobile telephony that all support a low-cost world-wide reach of business activities.

These waves of economic growth induced by technology innovation, whether real or construed, seem to peter out when the prevailing technology platforms mature and new disruptive technologies come to the scene through entrepreneurial efforts. That is, the global economy does not seem to revolve around a state of long-run economic equilibrium but is constantly disrupted by new technologies. On the face of it, the periodic waves of technology innovation appear to be accelerating, i.e., the *long waves* are becoming shorter than was the case with the first wave, from lasting around 50–60 years to covering time spans of 25–30 years. Hence, it is argued that we may be in a relatively short-lived fifth technology wave driven by computer software and digital networks with extended Internet connectivity and mobile communication capabilities. We are already witnessing what may be the sixth wave of technology innovation in the form of artificial intelligence (AI) and machine learning. The increased adoption of machine learning in technology products and platforms, whereby automated algorithms can learn from data and find insights without being pre-programmed, is driven by the exponential growth of processing power in accordance with Moore's law, the use of GPUs[1] particularly suited for deep machine learning, and increasing data storage capacity at declining costs thanks to cloud computing. Advances in computer vision, language processing, social cognition, and machine navigation create new products and services. These technologies can have major implications for the multinational corporation, driving a new wave of applications that can redefine the multinational consumer and enterprise markets. Together these technologies can facilitate global communication links and individual knowledge networks as the engine that can exploit collective intelligence and enable collaborative learning as the essential means to deal effectively with a turbulent globalized business world.

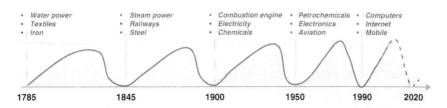

FIGURE 3.1 Schumpeter's waves of technology innovation and creative destruction.

Structural evolution

The conventional bureaucratic structure was introduced as an effective way of managing a given set of business activities and was organized as a *hierarchical structure* with top management situated at the pinnacle of power directing policies, practices and processes throughout the organization (Figure 3.2). A typical start-up firm would be headed by a founder whose strategic vision is leading the entire organization and all business activities associated with it (e.g., Mintzberg, 1973). As the organization expands its business volume it would face increasing demands for special competencies and expertise, moving it towards a *functional structure* with different operations and departmental units (e.g., Galbraith and Kazanjian, 1986). The continued expansion of a successful business was observed to form into larger corporate conglomerates with more or less related business activities, which would tend to drive the organization towards a *multidivisional structure* (M-form) as a way to contain distinct business activities within confined areas of executive oversight (Chandler, 1990, 1991). The related *internationalization* of business activities has typically been perceived as a gradual expansion first towards comparable neighboring national markets with largely similar cultural and institutional setups, to eventually extend across more and increasingly disparate geographical markets and regions.

As both the scope of diverse business activities and the geographical location of those businesses are extended across global markets, there may be a need to consider a divisional structure based on the degree of relatedness across different business activities and/or the diversity across regional geographical locations. In some situations this may call for a *matrix structure* with dual emphasis on significant business and geographical differences where each business entity consequently will report to two central executives, one responsible for specific business areas and another responsible for the geographical region. These deliberate organizational considerations reflect the mantra that *strategy precedes structure*. However, the opposite

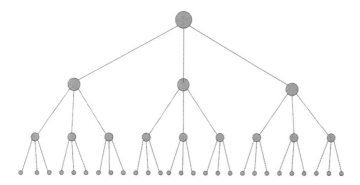

FIGURE 3.2 A simple top management focused hierarchical structure.

is also true, that is, the way the organization is structured influences how the strategy-making process is conducted. In other words, a hierarchical centralized organizational structure will make decisions in a different way than a flatter more decentralized structure where the latter arguably allows for more local responses to emerge. An organization that takes advantage of modern communication and information technologies will also be better able to support a structure of dispersed multinational activities and thus constitute an enabling structural factor behind a new phenomenon like *born global* among international start-up firms.

There has been a development away from conceptualizing the organization as a stand-alone entity to a more connected structure that depends on important actors inside as well as outside the firm, confined around major *stakeholder groups* like employees, managers, shareholders, customers, suppliers, financiers, regulators, etc. (Freeman, 1984). This reflects a realization that the ability to identify specific requirements of diverse stakeholders and provide the means to consider and deliver on those requirements is the key to sustainable performance and corporate longevity. It has also fostered ideas about the *boundaryless* organization, where communication and exchange of knowledge and insights among both internal and external constituents can enhance stakeholder relations and enable responses with higher value creation potential. It provides the basis for more open organizational structures with *permeable boundaries* that allow broader interaction and information exchanges across many diverse individuals, linked together in *virtual networks*.

The above perspective outlines the contours of the *networked organization* as a structure of independent companies, subsidiaries, or business units

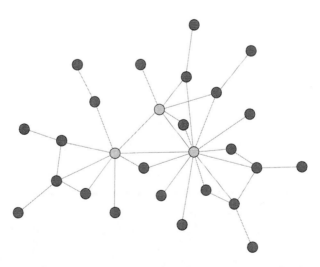

FIGURE 3.3 A basic network structure with dispersed communication nodes.

where employees and managers communicate freely, interact with each other, and engage in open collaboration to solve emerging problems and strategic issues. The network can comprise individuals both within business entities that operate as part of a large corporation, and business activities outsourced to other companies. The *network structure* is less hierarchical and generally more decentralized than conventional organizations where local managers and engaged individuals coordinate collaborative activities through informal communication links to attain the required mutual adjustments (Figure 3.3). This structure is more flexible because the local decentralized entities can take faster responsive decisions and generate bottom-up business ideas inspired by insights from direct contacts to important stakeholders. It constitutes a more fluid structural constellation where many complex relationships are managed informally around local business entities.

A particular dispersed organizational structure is referred to as collaborative innovation networks, defined as self-organizing groups of motivated individuals working together to achieve a common goal and sharing ideas and beliefs about a common cause (Gloor, 2005). A *collaborative innovation network* (COIN) is comprised of a virtual social team of self-motivated individuals that exchange information and knowledge in pursuit of a collective vision facilitated by Internet connectivity and IT-enhanced communication technologies (Figure 3.4). COIN members collaborate and share

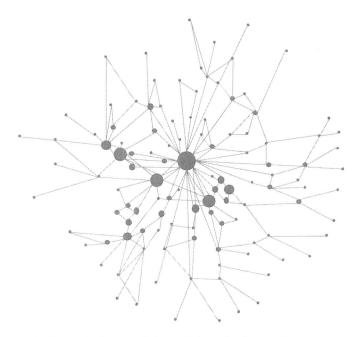

FIGURE 3.4 A distributed network for collaborative innovation.

information directly with each other without any directives or interference from organized hierarchies. They display the characteristics of open learning networks formed by independent like-minded individuals driven by ethical principles to achieve a higher purpose for common good. The structure builds on mutual trust among the individual participants where knowledge is accessible to everyone in the network based on principles of internal openness and transparency of information. The COIN is particularly conducive to the advancement of creative ideas and innovative developments based on collaborative learning that builds on the knowledge, experiences and insights of many diverse individuals.

Multinational structure

Maintaining business operations across a range of national markets provides a basis for obtaining scale and scope economic advantages where broader access to resources and more flexible sourcing of productive inputs can enable the realization of steady high performance outcomes (Bartlett and Ghoshal, 1989; Kogut, 1985; Tallman and Li, 1996). A flexible multinational structure of operations may enable a number of potential economic benefits including cross-border arbitrage opportunities (Teece, 1981), factor cost advantages (Govindarajan and Gupta, 2001) and location economies (Yip, 2001). If the *multinational structure* allows an ability to switch business volume between national operating entities it may also be possible to take advantage of changes in global price relations (Kogut and Kulatilaka, 1994; Rangan, 1998). It can allow the corporation to mitigate the effects of periodic swings in foreign exchange rates and economic exposures associated with changing demand conditions and relative factor costs in major economic regions (Kogut and Chang, 1996; Miller, 1998). Hence, business engagements across a multiplicity of market contexts can facilitate strategic moves to better manage the changing market conditions, exploiting unique multinational diversification opportunities (Kim, Hwang and Burgers, 1993; Reeb, Kwok and Baek, 1998).

The location of different business activities across multiple overseas markets with different product adaptations, technological applications, logistical structures, institutional settings, etc., provides differential market experiences and gives access to a unique set of diverse global resources that can be recombined in new ways to foster innovation and business development (Figure 3.5).

The networked multinational structure may constitute an extended form of *taper integration* where different corporate operations are located in the geographical regions that offer the most advantageous conditions for those particular functions. It may represent more multinational structures attempting to provide the operational and economic conditions to pursue a *global strategy* where economic efficiencies are optimized or pursuing a *transnational strategy* with built-in operational flexibilities to enable local responses. The finance function, for example, might be operating from an international

Geographic, product, and functional matrix organization

- Global strategy
- Transnational strategy   An extended form of 'taper integration'

FIGURE 3.5 A networked multinational structure.

financial center with direct access to global financial expertise, production might be placed in regions with advantageous labor conditions and distribution facilities, research and development centers could be located in specific technology hubs with close proximity to global research institutions, etc.

All of these corporate activities at different geographical locations criss-crossing the globe can be effectively integrated through the use of modern communication and information technologies. That is, the electronic bits that contain information on product design parameters, production specifications, sales orders, financial data, accounting reports, strategic plans, etc. can be transferred instantaneously, at virtually no variable costs, around the world. So, from an economic perspective there is no difference between maintaining an organizational structure confined to a narrow physical location and one that is extended throughout the globe with activities placed in different geographical regions. This obviously provides new opportunities for more optimal multinational structures of corporate business operations. On the other hand, one must also consider the potential challenges associated with administrative and managerial demands from conducting business activities in vastly different cultural and institutional settings and the potential impact from global economic and political events.

The multinational structure arguably provides a better basis for taking advantage of differences in conditions between major economic regions, thereby improving the ability to cope with various economic exposures and environmental changes. Building operational flexibilities along a global value-chain can install the possibilities to switch sourcing flows, business activities, and distribution channels between geographical locations as general demand conditions, factor prices, foreign exchange rates, etc. change over time (Kogut and Chang, 1996; Miller, 1998).

Furthermore, a multinational structure gives access to diverse skills, competencies, and market insights. It constitutes a versatile knowledge reservoir that offers the possibility to enhance business development efforts (Desouza and Evaristo, 2003; Mudambi, 2002). The implied ability to mobilize and recombine different knowledge-based resources in new valuable unique firm-specific innovative endeavors holds promise as a source for extracting sustainable excess returns (Barney, 1991).

Hence, a multinational structure can provide a unique platform for creating global business opportunities for the corporation that extend the range of available strategic options and increase maneuverability in the face of ongoing changes in the competitive environment (McGrath et al., 2004; Tong and Reuer, 2007). The multinational business opportunities can be conceived as a portfolio of growth options to be managed dynamically and nurtured for ongoing development and eventual implementation, if the competitive conditions become favorable for exercise (Luehrman, 1998; Tong and Reuer, 2007). A suitably composed portfolio of international strategic options can increase available decision alternatives for future execution and thereby improve the ability to deal with emerging changes in global market conditions.

However, some availability of organizational slack as surplus resources is required to fuel new business development activities (Nohria and Gulati, 1996). Slack resources also affect the ability to maintain the multinational flexibilities that underpin the ability to respond to environmental changes and enable strategic response capabilities (Bettis and Hitt, 1995; Greenley and Oktemgil, 1998). Slack is conceived as resources committed in excess of those required to accomplish the basic operational tasks and thus represent incremental resources that can be drawn on to support sudden needs for immediate responses and innovative initiatives (Nohria and Guhlati, 1996).

The ability to engage in innovative activities in ongoing development efforts thrives on slack and financial resources (Nohria and Gulati, 1996). Accordingly, it is argued that "slack resources ... allow a company to adapt to environmental change, by providing the means for achieving flexibility in developing strategy options to pursue opportunities" (Greenley and Oktemgil, 1998). In other words, slack resources are an antecedent to innovation where cash balances and capital reserves serve to finance development and eventual investment in multinational business opportunities.

The viability of multinational business opportunities is expressed by the net present value of the future cash flows ascribed to the implied business ventures, which is held against the front-end investment required to execute the business propositions (Dixit and Pindyck, 1994; Trigeorgis, 1996). Hence, there is both a need to invest resources in the development of business opportunities, and a need for financial resources to be readily available for investing in the execution of the underlying multinational business projects. Capital reserves in the form of retained earnings can be conceived of as slack, enabling funding for option execution (Greenley and Oktemgil, 1998). That is, a certain amount of slack resources is required to pursue research and development efforts and eventually exploit those business opportunities and adapt the multinational organization to the changing global context.

The resulting performance implications of a multinational structure should be expressed as a positive relationship to the upside business potential realized by the organization and a negative relationship to adverse risk outcomes. However, it is also apparent that the performance effects of multinationality to a large extent must derive from an enhanced capacity for innovation, which in turn is influenced by the availability of slack resources such as cash balances and capital reserves.

Therefore, the multinational performance dynamic drives on sufficient organizational slack and capital reserves made available for innovation and responsiveness purposes that, together with the diverse knowledge characteristics of the multinational organization, enhances upside business opportunities and diverts downside risk outcomes. So, financial slack together with diversity in multinational resources and knowledge induce innovation and when the innovative efforts are supported by capital reserves they can lead to a significantly higher multinational performance.

It cannot be claimed that the multinational structure by itself is associated with significant risk diversification effects above and beyond influences from organizational size and the presence of capital reserve buffers (Andersen, 2011), a claim that is counter to the risk diversification effects reported in other studies (e.g., Kim, Hwang & Burgers, 1993). Conversely, there is no indication that multinationality induces higher downside risk outcomes that would suggest internationalization as being a particularly risky strategic move (e.g., Reeb et al., 1998).

Hence, advantageous risk and performance effects from a multinational structure derive from global resource diversity that enhances innovation and enables an ability to exploit the upside potential of new business opportunities provided it can be fueled by financial slack and capital reserves. So, a multinational structure has incremental performance-enhancing effects when pursued in conjunction with investment in innovation and a prudent capital structure that provides sufficient financial slack to induce business development efforts and an organizational setting that supports innovative initiatives. In short, the multinational performance effects can largely be ascribed to corporate innovation activities, a supportive organizational structure, and the availability of sufficient financial slack.

A multinational organization, with operations in different national environments, provides access to diverse skills, competencies and insights that can fuel processes of recombining existing pieces of knowledge into new useful knowledge (Barkema et al., 1996; Nonaka, 1994). The implied knowledge management capabilities provide the capacity to develop and exploit multinational strategic options by investing in innovation (Desouza and Evaristo, 2003; Kogut and Kulatilaka, 1994; Mudambi, 2002). The strategic options linked to multinational business opportunities in turn enhance the ability to exploit upside gains and fend off adverse effects that arise from the changing global market context (Swart and Kinnie, 2003).

Effective responses in multinational subsidiaries

The multinational innovation potential is driven by the diversity in market knowledge, insights and capabilities that is extended by a corporate presence of business activities located in different national market settings. Hence, the multinational strategy-making process can be linked to the in-coming and out-going knowledge flows associated with business activities carried out in the local subsidiaries (Gupta and Govindarajan, 1991). Here, the underlying idea is that the multinational presence gives access to a broader diversity of resources, knowledge and revenue streams that can contribute to new business development (e.g., Doukas and Kan, 2006; Govindarajan and Gupta, 2001). These potential multinational performance advantages, based on the ability to exploit multinational opportunities, is real but is also industry-specific and is particularly pronounced in knowledge-based information-intense industry contexts (Andersen, 2012). So multinational organizations can take advantage of dispersed knowledge-based resources but are also sensitive to potentially adverse effects associated with capital-intensive business activities where substantial financial resources may be bound to irreversible investments in productive assets. To the extent that the multinational business activities depend on these types of long-term investment commitments, the productive assets should as far as possible be built around flexible and resilient structures that can accommodate local market changes and potential economic and political events in the global market context.

This is not unlike the considerations made from a strategic management perspective, which shows how central direction informed by rational analytical considerations of the competitive environment, combined with decentralized responses at dispersed business entities, is associated with superior performance outcomes (see Chapter 1). This interactive strategy-making model is facilitated by effective internal communication links between managers at different hierarchical levels and among managers located in local business entities. The generic framework can be described as a dynamic interaction between rational analytical reasoning at the corporate center and ongoing responses carried out by individuals located in business entities in the periphery, close to the important external stakeholders. That is, the central and peripheral processes rely on effective communication and information-processing capabilities that combine the central to the peripheral entities as well as allowing for ongoing information exchange between peripheral business entities (Figure 3.6).

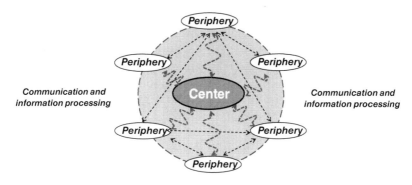

FIGURE 3.6   Communication links and interaction between the periphery and corporate center.

The multinational organization has been conceptualized as an *intra-organizational business network* comprising the combined activities across interlinked local business entities (Bartlett and Ghoshal, 1989; Hedlund, 1986). This perspective has pointed to the potentially important role of the overseas subsidiaries and their ability to act in their own interests, which has inspired a research stream focused on the strategic importance of subsidiary responsiveness. The autonomous initiatives taken by overseas subsidiaries have been defined as "entrepreneurial activities carried out by foreign subsidiaries of multinational corporations" (Birkinshaw and Ridderstråle, 1999: 14). These research efforts have analyzed how subsidiaries can develop important capabilities from their engagements across various external networks (Andersson et al., 2002, 2007) thereby influencing the overarching strategy of the multinational organization by taking initiatives on their own.

This research considers the direct and indirect effects of subsidiary autonomy where the headquarters may delegate decision-making power voluntarily for strategic reasons with authority obtained from headquarters because there is substantial dependence on unique knowledge and capabilities in the respective subsidiaries. Hence, the overseas subsidiaries can have substantial strategic influence and maintain decision-making power within the multinational organization, which could allow them to abandon the roles initially ascribed to them by the headquarters (Dörrenbacher and Gammelgaard, 2010; Gammelgaard, 2009). That is, the multinational subsidiaries can eventually drive an idiosyncratic strategy-making process adapted to the specific requirements of their local markets. This can, in turn, provide a basis for developing new strategic initiatives locally that respond directly to emerging threats and opportunities observed directly in the national and regional markets. Thus, it is generally known that various types of knowledge absorbed from different host countries can be useful for innovative initiatives in the local subsidiaries (Phene and Almeida, 2008). This can constitute a distinctive organizational capability that develops and adapts organizational activities over time by integrating knowledge residing both inside and outside the boundaries of the multinational organization. It can reflect a unique firm-specific capacity because "not all firms will be able to combine knowledge from different source locations to generate novel innovations" (Berry, 2014). That is, some multinational organizations are able to develop basic interactive relationships that have evolved from a tradition of integrated cross-border manufacturing or other types of multinational collaborative experiences.

However, the foreign subsidiaries will always to some extent be guided by the general guidelines provided by the corporate headquarters originating from the initial formation of the multinational structure but may change character over time based on ongoing experiences and concrete business outcomes. Therefore, the local subsidiaries can obtain a *mandate from headquarters* reflecting the intended strategy imposed by top management in line with the corporate mission and outlining specific actions to achieve in accordance with the overarching strategic direction communicated broadly throughout the multinational organization. This general strategic direction imposed by headquarters provides guidance to ongoing business activities and operational execution and provides the local managers with a general policy direction to guide their decisions as they respond to changing conditions in the local markets. It may serve to ensure that local initiatives are carried out more or less in line with the overarching purpose of the corporation, so subsidiary projects are commensurate with the general multinational strategy of the corporation. This can provide support for local responses adapting to emerging market needs while ensuring a certain alignment of activities around the corporate purpose that may enhance the decision-making authority delegated to local subsidiary managers.

If we conceive multinational strategy-making as a sequence of resource committing decisions made across hierarchical levels, functional entities, and geographic locations in the multinational organization, the corporate decision structure will have a direct bearing on how strategic initiatives are executed. With a more decentralized decision structure, the corporate headquarters can implement communication and information-processing systems that support dispersed decision makers by facilitating the informal exchange of information across hierarchical levels, functional areas, and geographical locations, giving access to all policy and management reports. The delegation of decision-making power to overseas subsidiaries can identify two different forms of *autonomy*. With one type of autonomy the local decisions can determine which business projects to pursue that will have a direct bearing on the subsidiary's assigned activities. We refer to this as *strategic autonomy*. Another type of autonomy provides local managers with the freedom to manage human resources and staffing decisions that affect the subsidiary's operational performance with respect to assigned business activities in view of the local market conditions. We refer to this as *operational autonomy*.

Hence, *operational autonomy* is defined as decision-making authority on hiring, firing, and training local staff, given to local managers with respect to subsidiary execution of local business activities and cooperative arrangements. The decision rights on issues like "hiring and firing of staff" and "training programs" at the subsidiary level are important for the way the subsidiary executes its ongoing business activities, carries out new projects, and develops knowledge-based competencies for future projects and business development. Local autonomy to manage human resources should have a positive effect on performance because decisions are made closer to the affected activity where the relevant information is available. This is particularly true in the case of downstream activities where goods and services may cater to culturally diverse business environments. Furthermore, autonomy to engage in local cooperative business engagements should increase the subsidiary's ability to respond to and exploit new opportunities that arise in the local market context, which should improve subsidiary performance and hence the corporate outcomes (Andersson et al., 2002).

By comparison *strategic autonomy* is defined as decision-making authority delegated to the local subsidiary managers with respect to the direction of local business activities, engagement in new business projects, and setting the related budgeting targets to be achieved by the subsidiary. Strategic autonomy provides the freedom to pursue local initiatives of potential strategic significance as local managers are empowered to commit and apply the needed resources towards their own strategic projects. It includes decision-making power in matters that affect "overall direction of subsidiary" and "new business projects" that may have a direct influence on the realized strategy. Local decisions taken with respect to subsidiary direction and new business projects will affect the role of the subsidiary in the multinational organization and influence the official corporate role of the subsidiary. Maintaining local strategic autonomy can increase the ability to respond to changes in local market conditions. However, it may also run counter to the overarching coordination aims of corporate activities and thus will rely on the effectiveness of mutual adjustments made across self-established networks of collaborative partnerships (e.g., Bartlett and Ghoshal, 1989).

To make autonomous decisions work effectively there is a need for internal communication and information capabilities that will allow different functional managers to interact and coordinate things informally to execute dispersed actions. We, therefore, consider the extent to which *informal exchange relationships* can be exercised, consisting of an ability of subsidiary managers to build their own social networks for open communication and knowledge exchange. It is related to the delegation of authority, with some freedom of operations, and a culture of openness to share and exchange information among organizational actors. It is related to the extent to which local managers visit managers in other subsidiaries and participate in collaborative business meetings with other subsidiary managers. It constitutes informal personal contacts among individuals located in different subsidiaries where direct social interactions allow knowledge and insights to be freely exchanged. The extent to which information and knowledge can be exchanged freely provides the means to develop better solutions dealing with emerging challenges and develop business opportunities incorporating expertise and insights from many different collaborating individuals. The open exchange of knowledge through personal informal contacts and networks can facilitate innovation and opportunity-seeking behaviors throughout the multinational organization. The informal communication capabilities with actors both inside and outside the organization can facilitate better adaptive solutions to changing market needs and coordinate interdependent responsive initiatives through mutual adjustments among the involved individuals.

The conceptualization of a networked multinational organization comprised of business activities pursued across interlinked subsidiaries is illustrated in Figure 3.7. The headquarters provides some direction to local subsidiaries by providing a formal strategic mandate. The local subsidiaries act fairly autonomously within this mandate and may be able to take both operational and strategic decisions on their own. However, the actions taken by the local subsidiaries are coordinated through mutual adjustments between involved business entities and ongoing interaction between subsidiaries and headquarters. This implied communication and knowledge exchange is carried out through informal exchange relationships constituted by personal social contacts formed and maintained through individual initiatives and their social interaction.

The subsidiary business activities are linked across autonomous subsidiary initiatives. The local subsidiaries pursue autonomous initiatives in line

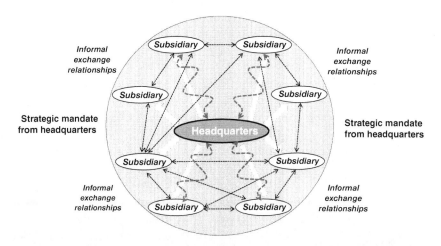

FIGURE 3.7   Strategic mandate from headquarters and informal communication between subsidiaries.

with their strategic mandate, with the intention of optimizing long-term subsidiary performance and where potential positive spillover effects between the intertwined subsidiary relationships also may exert an influence on the total multinational corporate performance. In this set-up the economic efficiency and value creation potential of the multinational organization will be enhanced both by *operational autonomy* and *strategic mandate from headquarters.* Similarly, the presence of *informal exchange relationships* will have a positive effect on multinational performance outcomes. The existence of *strategic autonomy* does not generally seem to have any impact on performance. Only when strategic autonomy is combined with *informal exchange relationships* does it have a positive effect on multinational performance.

These considerations show the importance of combining central direction from headquarters with the delegation of decision-making power to the subsidiary management. However, it suggests a more nuanced perspective than discussed in the generic strategy-making model. That is, operational autonomy is universally a good proposition and the prevalence of informal exchange relationships as effective means to deal with turbulent conditions of the global market context is in line with the strategic responsiveness arguments. However, we cannot say that strategic autonomy is always a good proposition for the overseas subsidiaries, since it is contingent on informal exchange relationships as a condition for effective multinational outcomes. Hence, strategic autonomy can have positive performance effects when subsidiary managers engage in open informal communication with headquarters and other subsidiary managers to mutually coordinate the business initiatives.

Summary

Global economic growth seems driven by narrowing periodic waves of technology innovation and creative destruction where new network-based multinational structures emerge to deal with an increasingly turbulent business context. The networked multinational structure can exploit global economic efficiencies while enabling local responses to specific developments in national markets if the overseas subsidiaries operate conjointly under a strategic mandate from headquarters and have broad autonomy enhanced by open communication links across the network.

Note

1 GPU (*Graphics Processing Unit*) is a chip processor that performs computation-intensive tasks, transforming objects into 3D, which has major design and development applications.

References

Andersen, T. J. (2011). The risk implications of multinational enterprise, *International Journal of Organizational Analysis*, **19**(1): 49–70.

Andersen, T. J. (2012). Multinational risk and performance outcomes: Effects of knowledge intensity and industry context. *International Business Review*, **21**: 239–252.

Andersson, U., Forsgren, M. and Holm, U. (2002). The strategic impact of external networks: Subsidiary performance and competence development in the multinational corporation. *Strategic Management Journal*, **23**(11): 979–996.

Andersson, U., Forsgren, M. and Holm, U. (2007). Balancing subsidiary influence in the federative MNC: A business network view. *Journal of International Business Studies*, **38**(5): 802–818.

Barkema, H. G., Bell, J. H. and Pennings, J. M. (1996). Foreign entry, cultural barriers, and learning. *Strategic Management Journal*, **17**(2): 151–166.

Barney, J. (1991). Firm resources and sustained competitive advantage. *Journal of Management*, **17**(1): 99–120.

Barney, J. B. (1986). Strategic factor markets: Expectations, luck, and business strategy. *Management Science*, **32**(10): 1231–1241.

Bartlett, C. and Ghoshal, S. (1989). *The Transnational Corporation*. New York, NY: The Free Press.

Berry, H. (2014). Global integration and innovation: Multicountry knowledge generation within MNCs. *Strategic Management Journal*, **35**: 869–890.

Bettis, R. A. and Hitt, M. A. (1995). The new competitive landscape. *Strategic Management Journal*, **16**(S1): 7–19.

Birkinshaw, J. and Ridderstråle, J. (1999). Fighting the corporate immune system: A process study of subsidiary initiatives in multinational corporations. *International Business Review*, **8**(2): 149–180.

Chandler, A. D. (1990). *Strategy and Structure: Chapters in the History of the Industrial Enterprise* (vol. 120). Cambridge, UK: MIT Press.

Chandler, A. D. (1991). The functions of the HQ unit in the multibusiness firm. *Strategic Management Journal*, **12**(S2): 31–50.

Chen, M. J. (1996). Competitor analysis and interfirm rivalry: Toward a theoretical integration. *Academy of Management Review*, **21**(1): 100–134.

Desouza, K. and Evaristo, R. (2003). Global knowledge management strategies. *European Management Journal*, **21**(1): 62–67.

Dixit, A. K. and Pindyck, R. S. (1994). *Investment Under Uncertainty*. Princeton, NJ: Princeton University Press.

Dörrenbächer, C. and Gammelgaard, J. (2010). Multinational corporations, interorganizational networks and subsidiary charter removals. *Journal of World Business*, **45**(3): 206–216.

Doukas, J. A. and Kan, O. B. (2006). Does global diversification destroy firm value? *Journal of International Business Studies*, **37**(3): 352–371.

Freeman, R. E. (1984). *Strategic Management: A stakeholder approach*. Boston, MA: Pitman.

Galbraith, J. R. and Kazanjian, R. K. (1986). *Strategy Implementation: Structure, Systems and Process*. St Paul, MN: West.

Gammelgaard, J. (2009). Issue selling and bargaining power in intrafirm competition: The differentiating impact of the subsidiary management composition. *Competition & Change*, **13**(3): 214–228.

Gloor, P. (2005). *Swarm Creativity: Competitive Advantage Through Collaborative Innovation Networks*. Oxford, UK: Oxford University Press.

Govindarajan, V. and Gupta, A. K. (2001). *The Quest for Global Dominance: Transforming Global Presence into Global Competitive Advantage*. San Francisco, CA: Jossey-Bass.

Greenley, G. E. and Oktemgil, M. (1998). A comparison of slack resources in high and low performing British companies. *Journal of Management Studies*, **35**(3): 377–398.

Gupta, A. K. and Govindarajan, V. (1991). Knowledge flows and the structure of control within multinational corporations. *Academy of Management Review*, **16**(4): 768–792.

Hedlund, G. (1986). The hypermodern MNC – a heterarchy? *Human Resource Management*, **25**(1): 9–35.

Kim, W. C., Hwang, P. and Burgers, W. P. (1993). Multinationals' diversification and the risk-return trade-off. *Strategic Management Journal*, **14**(4): 275–286.

Kogut, B. (1985). Designing global strategies: Comparative and competitive value-added chains. *Sloan Management Review*, **26**(4): 15–28.

Kogut, B. and Chang, S. J. (1996). Platform investments and volatile exchange rates: Direct investment in the US by Japanese electronic companies. *The Review of Economics and Statistics*, 221–231.

Kogut, B. and Kulatilaka, N. (1994). Operating flexibility, global manufacturing, and the option value of a multinational network. *Management Science*, **40**(1): 123–139.

Luehrman, T. A. (1998). Strategy as a portfolio of real options. *Harvard Business Review*, **76**: 89–101.

McGrath, R. G., Ferrier, W. J. and Mendelow, A. L. (2004). Real options as engines of choice and heterogeneity. *Academy of Management Review*, **29**(1): 86–101.

Miller, K. D. (1998). Economic exposure and integrated risk management. *Strategic Management Journal*, **19**(5): 497–514.

Mintzberg, H. (1973). Strategy-making in three modes. *California Management Review*, **16**(2): 44–53.

Mudambi, R. (2002). Knowledge management in multinational firms. *Journal of International Management*, **8**(1): 1–9.

Nohria, N. and Gulati, R. (1996). Is slack good or bad for innovation? *Academy of Management Journal*, **39**(5): 1245–1264.

Nonaka, I. (1994). A dynamic theory of organizational knowledge creation. *Organization Science* **5**(1): 14–37.

Phene, A. and Almeida, P. (2008). Innovation in multinational subsidiaries: The role of knowledge assimilation and subsidiary capabilities, *Journal of International Business Studies*, **39**: 901–919.

Porter, M. E. (1980). *Competitive Strategy: Techniques for Analyzing Industries and Competitors*. New York, NY: Free Press.

Porter, M. E. (1985). *Competitive Advantage: Creating and Sustaining Superior Performance*. New York, NY: Free Press.

Porter, M. E. (2008). The five competitive forces that shape strategy. *Harvard Business Review*.

Rangan, S. (1998). Do multinationals operate flexibly? Theory and evidence. *Journal of International Business Studies*, **29**(2): 217–237.

Reeb, D. M., Kwok, C. C. and Baek, H. Y. (1998). Systematic risk of the multinational corporation. *Journal of International Business Studies*, **29**(2): 263–279.

Schumpeter, J. A. (1939). *Business Cycles: A Theoretical, Historical and Statistical Analysis of the Capitalist Process*. London, UK: McGraw-Hill.

Schumpeter, J. A. (1942). *Capitalism, Socialism and Democracy*. London: Routledge.

Swart, J. and Kinnie, N. (2003). Sharing knowledge in knowledge-intensive firms. *Human Resource Management Journal*, **13**(2): 60–75.

Tallman, S. and Li, J. (1996). Effects of international diversity and product diversity on the performance of multinational firms. *Academy of Management Journal*, **39**(1): 179–196.

Teece, D. J. (1981). Internal organization and economic performance: An empirical analysis of the profitability of principal firms. *The Journal of Industrial Economics*, **30**(2): 173–199.

Teece, D. J. (2007). Explicating dynamic capabilities: The nature and microfoundations of (sustainable) enterprise performance. *Strategic Management Journal*, **28**(13): 1319–1350.

Teece, D. J. (2010). Business models, business strategy and innovation. *Long Range Planning*, **43**(2): 172–194.

Teece, D. J., Pisano, G. and Shuen, A. (1997). Dynamic capabilities and strategic management. *Strategic Management Journal*, **18**(7): 509–533.

Thompson, W. R. (1990). Long waves: Technological innovation, and relative decline, *International Organization*, **44**(2): 201–233.

Tong, T. W. and Reuer, J. J. (2007). Real options in multinational corporations: Organizational challenges and risk implications. *Journal of International Business Studies*, **38**(2): 215–230.

Trigeorgis, L. (1996). *Real Options: Managerial Flexibility and Strategy in Resource Allocation*. Cambridge, MA: MIT Press.

Wernerfelt, B. (1984). The resource-based view of the firm. *Strategic Management Journal*, **5**(2): 171–180.

Yip, G. S. (2001). *Total Global Strategy*. Upper Saddle River, NJ: Prentice Hall PTR.

4

USING FRONTLINE STAKEHOLDERS TO SENSE THE ENVIRONMENT

Key points

- Multinational environmental scanning and sensing
- Sensing the local environments to gather global market intelligence
- Collecting the environmental sensing of frontline stakeholders

In this chapter we discuss the important role of the stakeholders that operate around the periphery (frontline) of the multinational organization as they sense important changes that emerge in the local markets where they are located. The updated insights captured by these *frontline stakeholders* can be collected and brought forward to the corporate headquarters as important input to inform discussions about adaptive moves in view of evolving changes in the global market.

Environmental scanning as the "activity of acquiring information" from the environment (Aguilar, 1967: 1) is a core activity that tries to gain insights into the changes that happen around the local business environments of the multinational corporation that can inform strategic decisions. Daft and Weick (1984) argue that organizational actions are the result of collecting and interpreting information from the surrounding business environment. By the time an organization takes action, the environment has already changed again and thereby triggered an ongoing cycle of organizational adaptation, information gathering, interpretation and adaptation. Scanning simply involves "an exposure to and perception of information" (Aguilar, 1967: 18) and is constituted by monitoring and data collection activities that precede organizational interpretation processes (Daft and Weick, 1984). Scanning does not necessarily have to result in organizational actions although scanning activity is inherent in the formulation of alternatives and selecting the "best" approach (Bourgeois and Eisenhardt, 1988; Dean and Sharfman, 1993; Fredrickson, 1984). So, scanning is a necessary but not a sufficient condition for managerial decision-making and the articulation of strategic moves (Hambrick, 1982).

Scanning is a dual activity that involves both looking for information (*searching*) and looking at information (*viewing*). The individual decision maker is exposed to the environmental information and search with no specific need in mind. The purpose is both to scan broadly and focus on specific information to possibly detect early signals of impending changes. Many and varied sources of information are considered with vast amounts of impressions being screened by individual cognitive processes. The graininess of information is rough and it is held in tacit form by engaged individuals where large parts of the information can be dropped from attention quickly, which makes individuals particularly sensitive to selected issues of change (Choo, 1999).

Teece (2007, 2012) introduces the term *sensing* in strategic management as a first fundamental element of three essential behavioural activities among individual decision makers. These activities include (1) identification and assessment of opportunities (sensing), (2) mobilization of resources to create the opportunities (seizing) from the sensing information, and (3) restructuring to execute the opportunities and capture value (transforming) from sensing. According to Teece (2007) the act of sensing includes both *searching* for changes and *viewing* such changes to assess opportunities for the organization. Subsequent managerial activities then use the sensed insights as updated information for decisions and transform it into managerial responses.

The ability to sense and use the sensed information has performance implications and, therefore, "must be performed expertly if the firm is to sustain itself as markets and technologies change" (Teece, 2012: 1396). That is, sensing can serve as a basis for strategic differentiation, firm heterogeneity, thereby creating competitive advantage. Teece (2007: 1323) argues that the enterprise will be vulnerable if the sensing, creative, and learning functions are only left to the cognitive traits of a few individuals, such as the corporate top management team. That is, people are attentive to different signals in the environment and can develop particular cognitive biases when perceiving the environment (Gilovich et al., 2002). As a result, the organization needs to consider a broad spectrum of individuals around the organization as possible sources of environmental sensing.

Helfat and Peteraf (2014) discuss the cognitive capabilities associated with sensing and show how sensing activities are linked to two related cognitive capabilities: perception and attention. They define perception according to the American Psychological Association (2009) as the mental activities or processes "that organize information (in the sensory image) and interpret it as having been produced by properties of (objects or) events in the external (three-dimensional) world." Attention is seen as being critical for perception because it determines which stimuli are recognized as "a state of focused awareness on a subset of available perceptual information" (American Psychological Association, 2009). However, the capacity for perception and attention varies across individuals where experts seemingly can perceive information within the domain of their expertise faster and more accurately than non-experts (Kahneman et al., 1982).

In the multinational organization such experts are often made up of stakeholders that operate around the periphery of the overseas business entities, be they employees, customers, or local partners. These frontline stakeholders constantly accumulate knowledge about the operational business conditions in that particular market context. The ongoing sensing information from different frontline stakeholders is able to capture ongoing developments that, when put together, can identify important emerging trends in the environment. In the turbulent global context, there are many uncertainties that can influence corporate performance, including changing customer needs, technology inventions, competitor moves, etc., all of which are in a constant state of flux of continuous changes. That is, the performance of the multinational organization is constantly affected by new competitor moves that put the profit streams of the incumbent firms at risk. Teece, Pisano and Shuen (1997) give some examples to illustrate how these trajectories may take form. For example, in microelectronics ongoing environmental changes might involve miniaturization, greater chip density and compression, or digitization of business processes supported by information and communication technology. However, the emerging trajectories can also be hard to discern, so there is a need for proactive sensing and seizing activities, where learning and interpretive activities can foster new business opportunities in the industry.

The important role of frontline stakeholders

In turbulent global markets the ability to obtain early signals and foresee competitive developments around the local subsidiaries is important for the development of effective responses. The environmental changes are typically sensed by the frontline stakeholders first, including employees, customers and business partners, because they constantly observe and accumulate insights about how the local business entities perform. These observations derive from interaction with colleagues, reading the media, engaging in industry networks and simply listening to common gossip. That is, the field data with updated local market insights from different frontline stakeholder groups can comprise useful information for ongoing decisions.

We can apply a stakeholder perspective to determine who are dependent on company performance and conversely who the company depends on for the ability to achieve successful outcomes. The stakeholder concept was introduced in the 1960s by the Stanford Research Institute to stress the importance of employees, managers, customers, suppliers, partners and society at large in gaining sustainable competitive advantage and not just adopting a narrow shareholder perspective. Therefore, it is essential to determine corporate objectives that can be supported by the firm's major stakeholders to create a common interest and enhance collaboration that can facilitate long-term success (Freeman and McVea, 2001). For example, competitive market information sensed by local stakeholder groups can support successful market entry strategies as part of a strategy to internationalize corporate business activities. Hence, the adoption of a stakeholder perspective while gaining updated information from essential frontline stakeholders to inform ongoing corporate decisions improves the chances that the multinational organization can stay its strategic course.

Strategic decision-making in multinational organizations is typically seen as a top-management-driven activity at corporate headquarters (Andrews, 1971; Ansoff, 1965; Chandler, 1962). However, many corporations are increasingly focusing on flexible learning based on participative decision-making approaches and increased empowerment of local managers (e.g., Cotton et al., 1988; Mintzberg, 1989). Hence, fast and effective strategic decisions consider updated insights from diverse stakeholders with relevant expertise (Eisenhardt, 1989). That is, different frontline employees engaged in the execution of daily business activities sense the often subtle changes in competitive conditions within the local market context that can serve to identify emerging risks and opportunities which otherwise may be overlooked (Figure 4.1).

Top management and middle managers are more remote from the daily business transactions and are not exposed directly to ongoing events and as a consequence they are less precise in their observations and interpretations of environmental changes that often are seen first on the frontline.

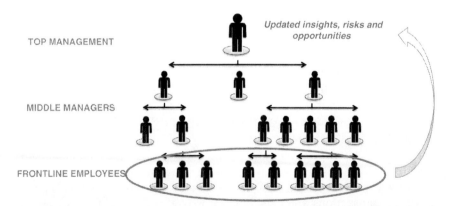

FIGURE 4.1 Collecting sensed environmental observations from frontline stakeholders.

All the while, the executives in top management develop *dominant logics* based on prior experiences that can become out of tune with reality, potentially making them unsuited to inform current decisions under changing environmental conditions (Bettis and Prahalad, 1995; Prahalad and Bettis, 1986). The presence of dominant logics means that the central decision makers at the corporate headquarters may lock the company into thinking about operating in only one way. Hence, Prahalad and Bettis (1986) suggest that the executive decisions made at headquarters will depend on the cognitive orientation of the top managers at the corporate center. However, if the corporate decision makers have a narrow and potentially biased perception of the competitive environment it impedes the discussions about proper ways to respond to the changing conditions. Moreover, it can hinder a free flow of information and ideas and stifle creativity to the detriment of the innovative search for effective responses to environmental changes. Individuals within (and around) organizations can also institutionalize particular interpretations of the environment, influenced by dominant cues from their networks (Levine and Kurzban, 2006; Levine and Zajac, 2008; Prato and Stark, 2013). Hence, it is the frontline stakeholders who must, on an ongoing basis, update the executives at headquarters on local market developments to enable proactive corporate responses. This builds on the premise that frontline stakeholders like employees, customers and partners are the first to sense conditional changes and the firm's ability to cope with those changes (Hallin, 2016; Hallin et al., 2013a, 2013b; Hallin and Lind, 2016).

The different stakeholder groups operating around the periphery or frontline of the corporate business entities have important updated insights about environmental developments in the form of weak signals sensed from their direct experiences in daily business transactions (Figure 4.2). These frontline stakeholders comprising frontline employees, customers and partners know the intricacies of their local markets well and gain updated insights about emerging environmental changes that can inform both local managers and executives at headquarters.

The environmental insights sensed by the frontline stakeholders in the multinational organization can be obtained from the people that manage the operations around the overseas business entities located in the national environmental contexts. They constitute frontline employees, customers and partners, that engage directly with each other in the daily business interactions, as essential stakeholder groups operating both inside and outside the local business entities and therefore perceive emerging changes immediately, or at least faster than anybody else. The sensed insights are grounded in daily experiences encountered from direct engagements in executing business transactions and consequently this sensing information tends to produce accuracy updated real-time information that can be used for corporate decision-making.

FIGURE 4.2 Essential frontline stakeholder groups around the organizational periphery.

The sensing information generated from frontline stakeholders tends to capture the perceived emerging changes before any other stakeholders and thus represent information that usually is un-available to top management and even to local managers in overseas subsidiaries. The sensed impressions of frontline stakeholders operating in the periphery of the multinational organization can be collected periodically to display important trends and changes in the global competitive context. That is, the sensed insights from different frontline stakeholder groups can provide unique updated information about the multinational environment to the corporate decision makers.

Sensing the multinational business environment

Multinational organizations can collect sensed environmental insights on an ongoing basis to inform forward-looking considerations with the aim to better understand the forces of change they must deal with to improve the competitive position of the corporation and enhance future performance. Hence, the ability of the multinational organization to adapt its business activities to ongoing changes in the business environment is influenced by the quality of updated sensing information made available from the frontline to interpret the environmental changes that are taking form. The sensing of frontline stakeholders constitutes a primary source of updated reconnaissance that can inform decisions about immediate responsive actions to environmental changes and observe the reactions to them. This captures the short-term effects of responsive initiatives as a source of ongoing trial and error learning from local experimentation. Hence, the multinational organization can learn about ongoing changes from immediate responses taken in the local markets by collecting updated sensing information from frontline employees on a regular basis. In the attempt to gain access to updated environmental sensing, the net may be cast more widely among a broader set of frontline constituents to capture all kinds of change signals from the multinational business environment. However, the sensing information can also focus on a specific concern or issue to gain updated information in support of concrete decisions. We may conceive of specific areas of global market reconnaissance related to broader environmental and business intelligence, competitor intelligence within the industry, and intelligence about the operational conduct of the multinational business entities.

Sensing for environmental and business intelligence relates to external market developments that may have an impact on the future performance of the multinational organization, often analyzed using the so-called PEST model (assessing changes in Political, Economic, Social and Technological conditions). Sensing for competitive intelligence is concerned with different variations of the five forces model (Porter, 1980). Additionally, the intelligence on operational conduct that has a direct effect on future performance in the multinational organization takes an internal look at the organization and the extent to which the corporation utilizes its internal resources effectively (e.g., Barney, 1991). See Chapter 1 for a quick review of the underlying industrial economics and resource-based rationales.

Sensing for environmental and business intelligence

Sensing to obtain intelligence about the general conditions that affect all sectors and industries in the global environment casts a wider net than that required to build competitor and competitive intelligence. The latter category is largely focused on conditions within a given industry context, e.g., assessed in a five forces framework. The *environmental* perspective covers all industries and considers the major macro-environmental factors that influence business conditions across the entire global market context typically assessed within a PEST framework (Figure 4.3). So, the PEST conditions circumscribe all industries in all economies although changes in the PEST factors can affect the competitive dynamic around the five forces in each industrial market in different ways that can be determined from comparative analysis.

The sensing information from frontline stakeholders can consider essential aspects of the external environment. Firms with overseas business entities can use this intelligence to identify local opportunities from the unique insights obtained from local stakeholders about changes in economic,

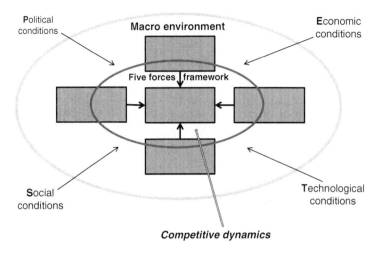

FIGURE 4.3 Analysis of external environmental factors (five forces and PEST).

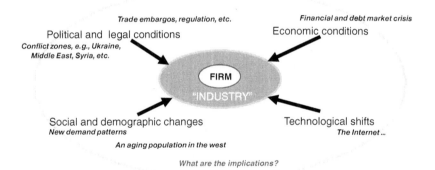

FIGURE 4.4 External environmental influences (industry and macro conditions).

political, legal, social, and demographic conditions (Li and Qian, 2013; Wang and Qian, 2011) that also can help top management at headquarters plan for the corporate strategy (Figure 4.4). The changes to these conditions can be abrupt, complex, dynamic, uncertain, unpredictable and unknown and therefore constitute phenomena that are very difficult or even impossible to foresee.

Sensing changes in new regulations and laws, business policies, political conflicts and wars can provide early signals and predictive indications about emergent macro-environmental conditions that will affect the performance outcomes of all the overseas business entities in the multinational organization. Sensing changes in the use of financial debt and savings products in the economy can similarly provide insights about emerging demand patterns and business models across the financial industry. Frontline stakeholders may also sense changing demand patterns caused by social and demographic changes in the underlying population that can lead to changes in taste, design, technology applications, institutional practices, etc. These subtle changes in the environmental context may cater to the development of new opportunities utilizing intimate knowledge about country-specific changes and trends that otherwise are hard to depict. Furthermore, it can be highly relevant to sense the emergence of possible technological disruptions that can prepare the multinational organization for future conditions and develop responsive initiatives and business opportunities that cater to the expected technological shifts.

The concept of *business* intelligence was introduced in information science (Luhn, 1958) and has been defined in numerous ways as an evolving concept. It can be seen as an umbrella term covering various uses of information technology, e.g., big data, crowdsourcing, online analytical processing, data mining, business performance management, data warehousing, artificial intelligence, statistical and research-based analytic tools. The development of business intelligence cuts across all industry and market contexts. The business intelligence practices apply information technologies across every sector of the global economy and can help corporate management plan strategic activities and integrate and process new information and updated intelligence to build competitive advantage.

The sensing among frontline stakeholders about new ways of using information technology is possibly one of the most visible opportunities to exploit environmental intelligence in the multinational organization. Frontline sensing can relate to social network interaction, trends to use various cloud and mobile devices, extended usage of the Internet, artificial intelligence, etc.

Sensing for competitive intelligence

The competitive conditions are reflected in the degree of rivalry between existing and potential competitors in the industry, illustrated in the five forces framework (Porter, 1979, 1980). The framework considers five important economic forces: supplier power, buyer power, threat of substitutes, threat of new entry and competitive rivalry, that influence the level of profitability in the industry. The sensing among frontline stakeholders about these influential economic forces within the specific industry context can provide updated intelligence about the competitive conditions and the firm's ability to develop or maintain competitive advantages. This, in turn, can be applied to assess the status of current and potential actors within the industry to gain intelligence on competitors and potential competitor responses. According to Michael Porter (Porter, 1980: 47) the objective of *competitor intelligence* is "to develop a profile of the nature and success of the likely strategy changes each competitor might make, each competitor's likely response to the range of feasible strategic moves that other firms could initiate, and each competitor's probable reaction to the range of industry changes and broader environmental shifts that might occur."

Thus, sensing to build competitor intelligence will include attention to the actions, behaviors, and options available to existing and potential competitors. Sensing can also benefit the *competitive intelligence*, which includes attention to national and international competitors as well as competitive conditions in particular industries or regions (Sutton, 1988).

Sensing of *supplier power* gives attention to increases and decreases in the number of suppliers to the key inputs of the company, the uniqueness of their products and services, the control over the local business entities, the cost of switching from one supplier to another, and so on. The fewer the supplier choices the multinational business entities have and the more they depend on specific product and service deliveries, the more power the suppliers exert over the multinational organization. The organization can also capture sensing of *buyer power*, e.g., gain insights about whether the buyers tend to drive prices down and understanding why they aim to do so. Such sensing may revolve around the number of consumers, the importance of current offerings to the local consumers, the cost they incur if they switch the products and services offered by the multinational organization to other competing suppliers, etc. If the local business entities only deal with few, powerful buyers, then the customers are more likely to dictate the commercial terms of business contracts.

It may also be relevant for the multinational organization to engage in sensing about the ability of customers to find alternative ways of obtaining comparable services and products as *substitutes* to those already offered by the company. For example, if the multinational organization offers unique software automating important operating processes, the buyers may substitute this software offering by engaging in manual processes or by outsourcing the processes to other business partners in the local market. If the sensing information suggests that it is easy to substitute the products and services offered by the company, then this situation will reduce the bargaining position of the multinational organization. Similarly, sensing with respect to the potential for *new entry* into the local markets can be useful because the bargaining position of the multinational organization is affected if other companies find it is becoming easy to enter into the local markets. The sensing of market entry of new competitors may consider the time, money, and competencies required to enter and compete effectively in those markets. For example, if there are no economies of scale in local operations or if there is limited protection for key technologies, then new competitors may more easily enter those markets, thereby weakening the bargaining position. Hence, it can be relevant to sense whether there are substantial changes to existing entry barriers in the local markets so the multinational organization can take precautions to preserve a favorable market position and pursue the development of new competitive advantages.

The considerations about competitive intelligence eventually entail a focus on the level of *competitive rivalry* that prevails within the industry and impending changes in the industry dynamic across the overseas markets where the company has existing activities or a potential future presence. The economic effects are linked to identifying what the potential number of local market competitors are or will be and how effectively their capabilities are utilized across the overseas locations. If the multinational organization has many competitors in all the major markets, and the competitors are able to offer equally attractive products and services, then the company will have little bargaining power and limited prestige to lever over the position in those markets. Hence, a high level of competitive rivalry across major overseas markets will reduce the corporate bargaining position vis-à-vis customers, suppliers, and other commercial partners who can more easily engage in other business relationships unless they obtain a really good deal at the expense of the multinational company. On the other hand, if the sensing information from the frontline stakeholders indicates that the level of rivalry across important overseas markets generally is dropping and the company retains a fairly unique market position, then it is a sign that the company has been able to respond and adapt its business activities to its favor.

Sensing for operational intelligence

Gaining updated insights or intelligence about the operational conduct across the overseas business entities of the multinational organization relates to the effectiveness with which the corporation manages and utilizes the global pool of available resources. This reflects an internal reconnaissance perspective aimed at getting early signals and intelligence on emerging changes in the operating effectiveness, process efficiencies, and other aspects of the organizational structure and operations (see Chapter 3). The literature on strategic and structural fit between the operations of the multinational organization and the current environmental context is developed both in the organization theory and strategic management literatures. Miller (1992) suggests an integrated risk management framework that can be applied to gain insight in various dimensions of the operational performance of companies through the sensing of such areas (Hallin and Lind, 2016).

Miller (1992: 312) argues that "uncertainty about the environment and organizational variables reduce the predictability of corporate performance." Such uncertainties can arise from both exogenous changes, as presented above in sensing for environmental and business intelligence and competitive intelligence, but also with respect to internal events such as behavioral choices or combinations of the three. Firm-specific variables may include operating, project management and behavioral conditions among stakeholders. Uncertainties surrounding operating conditions may prevail around internal effectiveness, innovativeness, flexibility, financial performance and capacity utilization. Updated intelligence in relation to project management can indicate ability to successfully complete projects, meeting the project deadlines as planned and remaining within budgeted project costs. Behavioral intelligence can inform about the state of staff performance, managerial effectiveness, team collaboration, word of mouth promotion by customers, stakeholder satisfaction among customers, suppliers and employees, commitment and loyalty to the corporation, etc.

As every subsidiary is unique, decision makers must cast the net wide and address the probing questions to their frontline stakeholders in general terms, e.g., "what are the unique capabilities for the subsidiary and for the multinational corporation as a whole that can impact future profits?" That is, the focus of the sensing activities regarding operational intelligence must try to uncover the most important environmental aspects representing the key uncertainties that can affect subsidiary and corporate performance in the immediate future time period.

Collecting sensing information from frontline stakeholders

The idea of imposing more decentralized decision structures and participatory processes that can engage and use locally held knowledge among frontline stakeholders as a way to better cope with environmental uncertainties has its roots in early discussions within the economics and social science fields (e.g., Ansoff, 1980; Hayek, 1945). The sensed updated information or intelligence among various frontline stakeholder groups can be identified and systematically collected as input for ongoing discussions and interpretation to gauge how key aspects of the global environmental context may be changing. The collection of this intelligence can use particular *information aggregation* mechanisms to structure and gather relevant information from multiple sources and analyze the information in accordance with specific objectives using modern Internet technologies. Institutions that provide this type of information-processing are typically referred to as service aggregators. In a broader sense, information intermediaries such as newspapers, magazines, professional journals, and the increasing use of big data and social media constitutes information aggregation, since they all represent mechanisms that collect information from multiple sources and disseminate it for convenient consumption. These types of aggregators tend to serve the general information needs in businesses, but lack the functionality of being designed for specific sensing purposes, e.g., building environmental and business intelligence, competitor intelligence or intelligence on internal operational conduct and performance (see Box 4.1).

BOX 4.1 Aggregating environmental intelligence from the frontline and collective intelligence

To extract dispersed intelligence about important environmental uncertainties a number of new techniques have emerged in recent years. The techniques seek to aggregate what is referred to as the "wisdom of the crowds" where information from a broader set of constituents is gathered and used to gain more precise predictions (Surowiecki, 2004; Wolfers and Zitzewitz, 2004). *Collective wisdom* is the ability of a population or a diverse group of individuals to make an accurate forecast of a future outcome or an accurate characterization of a current outcome.

Hong and Page (2001, 2004) identify the preconditions for the collective wisdom theoretically. They develop the assumptions that a diverse crowd including both novices and experts, individuals with diverse insights about an event, can outperform few experts in predicting the event as the average of their predictions will single out any errors in judgments (Hong and Page, 2001, 2004). That is, for "wisdom" to emerge, the group must be sophisticated and sufficiently diverse in order to be "smart," that is, be able to make good predictions. These perspectives on collective intelligence resonate with the idea of using a diverse group of frontline stakeholders to sense the external and operational environment to accumulate the collective wisdom of changes and so promote accuracy in strategic responsiveness by decision makers.

A practical example can illustrate the implications of aggregating predictions from frontline stakeholders. "Prediction markets" is a form of aggregation mechanism to capture the collective intelligence. The basic principle behind prediction markets is to create a market where a number of individuals can invest in a particular outcome of interest, such as a political or social event. The market is closed when the event occurs, the result will be displayed and participants win or lose based on the outcome and invested money (Borison and Hamm, 2010). In that way decision makers can achieve information from many more places than if they complement its model with single or few expert opinions, creating more reliable predictions.

For example, a prediction market includes a bet on whether the president who is elected in 2016 is Hillary Clinton. To bet on this outcome, participants can buy a "betting" contract that triggers a gain on a dollar if Hillary Clinton wins the election in 2016, and $ 0, if this does not happen. Depending on the outcome of the election in 2016, the price of this contract can be somewhat less than (or equal to) a dollar as a maximum gain of one dollar. For example, the market price of the contract could be quoted at $ 0.60, which represents the group's overall assessment of the likelihood that Hillary Clinton will win the election. Again these markets must engage a truly diverse set of knowledgeable participants to provide accurate predictions.

A few pioneering studies have demonstrated the importance of frontline stakeholders in national and global markets as important sources of environmental intelligence that can have a significant effect on corporate performance outcomes. The information aggregation mechanism collects the judgmental predictions of frontline stakeholders electronically and links them to actual corporate performance measures to validate their significance (Hallin, 2016; Hallin et al., 2013a, 2013b; Hallin and Lind, 2016). These studies indicate that frontline employees in particular have unique capabilities in predicting environmental change parameters that have significant short-term performance effects. These parameters can include various KPIs (key performance indicators) as well as more subjective indicators like team collaboration, managerial effectiveness and innovativeness, all of which can help identify specific issues in areas that can be addressed by managerial interventions and strategic actions.

The ability to gather essential intelligence from relevant diverse sources provides the means to develop processes for early warnings on emerging trends and possibly disruptive changes that can have wider strategic implications for the multinational organization. The concept of a *strategic issue management* (SIM) system has been introduced as a systematic procedure for early identification of impending environmental changes and orchestration of fast responses to deal with these changes that are linked both to the internal and external environments (Ansoff, 1980). The idea of information aggregation to collect intelligence from frontline stakeholders can support this process whereby early identification of impending changes can be formally captured and presented for consideration that otherwise would be dismissed and lost from sight in the long-cycled forward-looking strategic planning considerations.

SIM operates within the annual planning cycle as a real-time system that continuously receives and interprets intelligence to identify and monitor strategic issues throughout the year, which in practice may mean monthly reviews and updates of key strategic parameters. This requires continuous surveillance, both inside and outside the organization of environmental changes arising in between the annual planning reviews, to issue warnings and alerts when updated intelligence suggests that new strategic issues are emerging and need immediate attention and active consideration.

Ansoff (1980) refers to strategic issues as an impending uncertainty development that can happen either inside or outside of the organization, and that will have an effect on the firm's ability to meet its strategic objectives. It may constitute a positive uncertainty in the form of an emerging business opportunity to be grabbed as the environment evolves, or it may constitute an internal strength that can be exploited to the firm's advantage. Conversely, it may also be an unwelcome external threat, or an internal weakness, that can challenge the very survival of the firm. Such environmental opportunities and challenges in the environment can be related to the sensing capabilities of important frontline stakeholder groups operating around the periphery of the multinational organization because they offer the possibility of capturing current intelligence to inform SIM. This can be utilized with advantage because in turbulent global market contexts the environmental changes are often fast and unpredictable where a conventional planning system is incapable of fast identification and timely consideration of emerging strategic issues.

A SIM represents a systematic procedure for early identification and fast response to emerging strategic issues, in both the internal and external environments, that can benefit from the different types of competitive intelligence. Ansoff (1980: 134) argues that early identification can be assured in two basic ways:

- SIM is a "real time" mechanism constantly preoccupied with strategic issues throughout the year, which in practice means periodic (say monthly) reviews and updating of a strategic issues list.

- This is a continuous surveillance, both inside and outside the enterprise, to deal with "fast" issues that may arise in between reviews using a "red light" warning signal to alert management of the need for immediate action.

The responsibility for managing the system is assumed by top management at corporate headquarters with the resources and the authority to initiate prompt action without unnecessary delays if it is considered necessary. A formal SIM system has the potential advantage of cutting through the normal multinational corporate hierarchy to gain attention and get things done. Ansoff (1980) refers to expert employees as sensing individuals in the multinational organization that accumulate the environmental information and enable them to identify emerging strategic issues. This corresponds to the conceptualization of frontline stakeholders as important reservoirs of updated environmental intelligence that can be utilized in the decision-making process.

The role of top management is to assign responsibilities, for dealing with identified strategic issues of importance to the entire multinational corporation, to those business entities that are best equipped to deal with the underlying issue, even if this may reach across several hierarchical levels. The necessary resources are then assigned directly to those in charge of the responsive projects as project leaders that in turn report directly to top management at corporate headquarters. In this way, a SIM can become a responsive corporate management system where top management not only depends on a long-cycled forward-looking planning process but also can identify and deal with emerging events.

The idea about a strategic issue management system dates back to the early development of the strategy field but there is still a void in the theoretical and empirical foundations for these types of early warning systems and their effective integration into the strategy-making process in large multinational networks. The new IT facilitated mechanisms to aggregate stakeholder sensed information, like those described above, can be used to gather updated collective intelligence for managerial decisions. This way strategic issue management can thrive on updated frontline intelligence, creating a better balance between local decision-making and considerations for the strategic mandate from headquarters in the networked multinational organization.

Summary

Environmental scanning is important for multinational organizations operating in turbulent global markets for remaining alert to emerging changes of potential strategic significance. The collective sensing of changes in business conditions among major frontline stakeholder groups that operate around the corporate headquarters and overseas business entities is an important source of environmental intelligence. Different information aggregation techniques can be applied to collect and present the updated insights of these frontline stakeholders to inform strategic issue management systems and deal more effectively with environmental change.

References

Aguilar, F. J. (1967). *Scanning the Business Environment*. New York, NY: MacMillan.
American Psychological Association. (2009). Glossary of Psychological Terms.
Andrews, K. R. (1971). *The Concept of Corporate Strategy*. Homewood, IL: Richard D. Irwin.
Ansoff, H. I. (1965). *Corporate Strategy: An Analytic Approach to Business Policy for Growth and Expansion*. New York, NY: McGraw-Hill.
Ansoff, H. I. (1980). Strategic issue management. *Strategic Management Journal*, **1**: 131–148.
Barney, J. (1991). Firm resources and sustained competitive advantage. *Journal of Management*, **17**(1): 99–120.
Bettis, R. A. and Prahalad, C. K. (1995). The dominant logic: Retrospective and extension. *Strategic Management Journal*, **16**(1): 5–14.
Borison, A. and Hamm, G. (2010). Prediction markets: A new tool for strategic decision-making. *California Management Review*, **52**(4): 125–141.
Bourgeois, L. J. and Eisenhardt, K. (1988). Strategic decision processes in high velocity environments: Four cases in the microcomputer industry. *Management Science*, **34**: 816–835.
Chandler, A. D. (1962). *Strategy and Structure: Chapters in the History of the American Industrial Enterprise*. Cambridge, MA: MIT Press.
Choo, Chun Wei. (1999). The art of scanning the environment. *Bulletin of American Society for Information Science*, February/March.

Cotton, J. L., Vollrath, D. A., Froggatt, K. L., Lengnick-Hall, M. L. and Jennings, K. R. (1988). Employee participation: Diverse forms and different outcomes. *Academy of Management Review*, **13**: 18–22.

Daft, R. L. and Weick, K. E. (1984). Toward a model of organizations as interpretation systems. *Academy of Management Review*, **9**(2): 284–295.

Dean, J. W. Jr. and Sharfman, M. P. (1993). Does decision process matter? A study of strategic decision making effectiveness. *Academy of Management Journal*, **39**: 368–396.

Eisenhardt, K. M. (1989). Making fast strategic decision in high-velocity environments. *Academy of Management Review*, **32**(3): 543–576.

Fredrickson, J. W. (1984). The comprehensiveness of strategic decision processes: Extensions, observations, future directions. *Academy of Management Journal*, **27**: 445–466.

Freeman, R. E. and McVea, J. (2001). A stakeholder approach to strategic management. In: Hitt, M., Harrison, J. and Freeman, R. E. (eds.) *Handbook of Strategic Management*. Oxford, UK: Blackwell Publishing, 189–207.

Gilovich, T. D., Griffin, D. and Kahneman, D. (2002). *Heuristics and Biases: The Psychology of Intuitive Judgment*. New York, NY: Cambridge University Press.

Hallin, C. A. (2016). Aggregating predictions of operational uncertainties from the frontline: A new proactive risk management practice, in T. J. Andersen (ed.) *The Routledge Companion to Strategic Risk Management*. London, UK: Routledge.

Hallin, C. A. and Lind, A. S. (2016). Identification of strategic issues for crowd predictions. Paper presented at Collective Intelligence Conference, New York, NY.

Hallin, C. A., Andersen, T. J. and Tveterås, S. (2013a). Who are the better predictors: Frontline employees or executive managers? SMS 33rd Annual International Conference. Atlanta, GA: Strategic Management Society.

Hallin, C. A., Andersen, T. J. and Tveterås, S. (2013b). Fuzzy predictions for strategic decision making: A third-generation prediction market. CGSR Working Paper Series (2). Frederiksberg, Denmark: Copenhagen Business School.

Hambrick, D. C. (1982). Environmental scanning and organizational strategy. *Strategic Management Journal*, **3**: 159–174.

Hayek, F. A. (1945). The use of knowledge in society. *American Economic Review*, **35**(4): 519–530.

Helfat, C. E. and Peteraf, M. A. (2014). Managerial cognitive capabilities and the microfoundations of dynamic capabilities. *Strategic Management Journal*, **36**(6): 831–850.

Hong, L. and Page, S. (2001). Problem solving by heterogeneous agents. *Journal of Economic Theory*, **97**(1): 123–63.

Hong, L. and Page, S. (2004). Groups of diverse problem solvers can outperform groups of high-ability problem solvers. *Proceedings of the National Academy of Sciences*, **101**(46): 16385–16389.

Kahneman, D., Slovic, P. and Tversky, A. (1982). *Judgment Under Uncertainty: Heuristics and Biases*. New York, NY: Cambridge University Press.

Levine, S. S. and Kurzban, R. (2006). Explaining clustering in social networks: Towards an evolutionary theory of cascading benefits. *Managerial and Decision Economics*, **27**: 173–187.

Levine, S. S. and Zajac, E. J. (2008). When and where can institutionalization occur? The case of price bubbles in financial markets. Best Paper Proceedings, Academy of Management: Anaheim, California.

Li, J. T. and Qian, C. (2013). Principal-principal conflicts under weak institutions: A study of corporate takeovers in China. *Strategic Management Journal*, **34**: 498–508.

Luhn, H. P. (1958). Business Intelligence System. *IBM Journal of Research and Development*, **2**(4): 314–319.

Miller, K. D. (1992). A framework for integrated risk management in international business. *Journal of International Business Studies*, **23**(2): 311–331.

Mintzberg, H. .(1989). *Mintzberg on Management: Inside Our Strange World of Organizations*. New York, NY: Free Press.

Porter, M. E. (1979). How competitive forces shape strategy. *Harvard Business Review*, **58**(2): 21–38.

Porter, M. E. (1980). *Competitive Strategy: Techniques for Analyzing Industries and Competitors*. New York, NY: Free Press, 1980.

Prahalad, C. K. and Bettis, R. A. (1986). The dominant logic: A new linkage between diversity and performance. *Strategic Management Journal*, **7**(6): 485–501.

Prato, M. and Stark, D. (2013). Attention networks: A two-mode network view of valuation. Working paper, *Center on Organizational Innovation*. New York, NY: Columbia University.

Surowiecki, J. (2004). *The Wisdom of Crowds: Why the Many are Smarter than the Few and How Collective Wisdom Shapes Business, Economies, Societies, and Nations*. New York, NY: Doubleday.

Sutton, H. (1988). *Competitive Intelligence*. New York, NY: The Conference Board, Inc.

Teece, D. J. (2007). Explicating dynamic capabilities: The nature and microfoundations of (sustainable) enterprise performance. *Strategic Management Journal*, **28**(13): 1319–1350.

Teece, D. J. (2012). Dynamic capabilities: Routines versus entrepreneurial action. *Journal of Management Studies*, **49**(8): 1395–1401.

Teece, D. J., Pisano, G. and Shuen, A. (1997). Dynamic capabilities and strategic management. *Strategic Management Journal* **18**(7): 509–533.

Wang, H. and Qian, C. (2011). Corporate philanthropy and financial performance of Chinese firms: The roles of social expectations and political access. *Academy of Management Journal*, **54**(6): 1159–1181.

Wolfers, J. & Zitzewitz, E. 2004. Prediction markets. *The Journal of Economic Perspectives*, **18**(2): 107–126.

5

BALANCING A CORPORATE MANDATE WITH LOCAL RESPONSES

Key points

- The dynamics of fast and slow processes
- Combining central planning and local responses
- Internal communication and multinational knowledge creation
- Using subsidiary knowledge and collaborative learning
- Creating a global adaptive multinational corporation

The ability to develop multinational business opportunities and adapt the multinational organization to the changing conditions across global markets calls for a balance between the dual pressures of integration by pursuing an overarching corporate intent and emergent initiatives that respond to evolving local market requirements. It reflects a need for central coordination expressed in a strategic mandate from corporate headquarters, combined with an ability of local subsidiary managers to engage in autonomous responses that cater to new emerging business conditions.

The sustainable performance of a multinational corporation arguably derives from a strategy-making process orchestrated around an organizational structure that forms a dynamic system of forward-looking strategic reasoning and ongoing adaptive responses in the local markets. This ability to engage in dynamic responses to the changing conditions provides a way to retain the competitive advantage in a turbulent global business environment (e.g., Teece, 2007, 2014). A combined focus on proactive response behaviors disbursed throughout the organization and central direction to coordinate activities for economic optimization is quite consistent with concurrent calls for a balance between exploration and exploitation (March, 1991). Hence, the strategy literature has pointed to central planning as the means to gain scale and scope economies from a common direction, based on integrated and coordinated actions across multinational corporate activities. That is, the ability to accommodate emergent responses to changing conditions while pursuing long-term strategic intent is an important underpinning of the complex strategy-making process (Mintzberg and Waters, 1985).

Strategic adaptation and change processes in multinational organizations are typically conceived as a string of orderly preplanned activities to be implemented in accordance with an overarching analytically determined purpose (e.g., Hayes, 2007). In contrast to this rather conventional view, we see adaptive capabilities as being closely associated with the ability to take decentralized responses, attempting to explore new opportunities as they emerge in the local market contexts. The exploratory local responses generate experiential insights that can update managerial perceptions at the corporate headquarters about the competitive reality and inform the forward-looking strategy considerations. Such perspective resonates with a concept of *organizational becoming* (Tsoukas and Chia, 2002) where corporate activities evolve from dispersed responses, the effects from which help managers make sense of ongoing changes and their cognitive representation of future strategy. Some scholars talk about a gradual move away from formal hierarchies towards institutional frames of delegated authority, joint problem-solving and informal coordination of activities (Whitley, 2003).

Others talk about participative decision-making where dispersed decision-making power involves employees at all levels in flexible responses to immediate changes in their task environments, interacting directly with various stakeholders in concrete transactions (Cotton et al., 1988; Dachler and Wilpert, 1978; Miller and Monge, 1986; Locke and Schweiger, 1979; Wagner 1994). For example, Huy (2011) shows the importance of middle managers in the implementation of strategies introduced by the corporate headquarters. The participative decision-making view resonates with a depiction of strategy-making as the effect of actions taken by many engaged employees and managers where the organization can be seen to benefit from the motivational effects of increased employee involvement (Black and Gregersen, 2000). Even though the learning school of strategy has posed a strong challenge to conventional top-down-driven strategy views, the insights are largely based on anecdotal and case-based accounts with richly described examples. Hence, even though the integrative strategy perspective has received general recognition, we still do not have a full understanding of how the concrete top-down and bottom-up mechanisms interact to create effective strategic adaptation.

The following elaborates this interactive conceptual understanding of strategy-making in the multinational corporation and outlines a model of dynamic responsiveness characterized by structural features of strategic intent and emergence (see Chapter 1).

Fast and slow processes

To present a model of dynamic responsiveness, it is advantageous to consider that human cognition fundamentally is comprised of *fast processes* of multifaceted observations, responses, reactions and impressions from the surrounding world, and *slow processes* that ponder about the insights gained from the many encounters with the surroundings (Andersen and Fredens, 2013). The combination of fast and slow processes provides a better understanding of the dynamic processes as the means to assess the changing conditions in a way that gives meaning and purpose to subsequent actions taken in view of the turbulent business context. The conditions that surround many current events and evolving developments produce updated observations in fast ongoing processes and the various impressions in turn can be interpreted and projected forward in slow time-consuming thinking processes. The interdependent nature of combined fast and slow information-processing capabilities forms a *dynamic system* of sensed impressions, responses, experiential insights and adaptive moves for longer-term purposes.

We can apply this dynamic system of fast–slow information-processing to better understand the multiplicity of actions and interactions that take place among individuals in different parts of a multinational corporation. The individuals acting at the operational frontline on the edge of the organizational periphery are the ones that execute all the daily transactions, observe emerging events first-hand, and gain experiences from the things that happen and the way stakeholders react to them through direct involvement. All these impressions provide a good sense of how conditions are changing in the evolving business environment, including their potential consequences, and thereby create a deeper understanding of how the environmental context is changing based on many current experiential insights and related discussions with peers and external contacts linked to the individual network. From an organizational perspective the diverse experiences and insights among many dispersed individuals can be collected and made available as updated information to be considered in periodic forward-looking deliberations at the corporate center, often referred to as strategic planning.

In the conventional strategy literature, the strategic planning considerations are seen over a ten-year horizon or longer (e.g., Ansoff, 1965). However, due to the turbulent nature of the fast changing global business environment, the strategic planning horizon of multinational corporations has shortened significantly. The strategic planning process has become even more dependent on the volatile nature of many industry environments. For example, the oil industry has traditionally held relatively few strategic surprises for strategists. While the environment has changed at times dramatically, it has happened in relatively foreseeable ways. That is, strategic planners know, for instance, that global supply will rise and fall as geopolitical forces play out and new resources are discovered and exploited. Strategic planners are also aware that demand will rise and fall with incomes, GDPs, weather conditions, and the like. In contrast, the changes in the Internet software industry would appear chaotic for an oil industry strategist because innovative ventures and new companies pop up frequently, often month by month, seemingly out of nowhere, and the pace at which companies build or lose volume and market share can be head-spinning. Major players such as Microsoft, Google and Facebook can, without much warning, introduce a new platform or standard that fundamentally alters the basis of competition (Reeves et al., 2012). That is, the competitive advantage of overseas subsidiaries comes from reading and responding to local and global signals faster than the rivals, adapting quickly to change, capitalizing on technology leadership to enhance competitive strengths. So, the ability to gain local market insights on the business must happen regularly to support faster and more frequent analytical processes at the corporate headquarters. In contrast, gaining current market insights in the oil industry may not need instantaneous updates but could possibly happen only on a monthly basis. Hence, the insights about environmental changes from local subsidiaries can be used to update forward-looking analyses at corporate headquarters where the frequency of information-processing is geared to the level of turbulence in the specific industry.

We can use a brain metaphor where the human mind operates a combined fast and slow processing system as a theoretical representation of the dynamic between fast and slow strategy-making processes in multinational corporations. Here fast impressions from many different overseas business activities provide current updates on environmental developments that can be interpreted in the forward-looking analytical considerations (Figure 5.1). Individual observations of environmental changes from decentralized responsive actions in organizational sub-groups combined with central evaluations of these experiential insights provide updated cognition about the evolving state of the environment. Hence, effective organizations enable ongoing observations from responsive actions that experiment with the way things can be done and encourage intense internal communication that feeds into forward-looking multinational strategy considerations around top management at corporate headquarters.

The updated human cognition about the changing environmental context is formed by many different impressions triggered by active senses scattered throughout the body that are sent through fast information channels managed by the amygdala and hippocampus and forwarded to the frontal lobes where the unique center for reasoning is located. Here the slow process of interpreting the many collected pieces of information is carried out over time to form an updated perception of the changing context by imagining future contexts through imagined extrapolations of trends and possible actions simulated into the future as a basis for evaluating the best actions going forward.

The management of strategic direction is often perceived as a cyclical process of analytical planning, execution through actions, and ongoing

Fast responses/observations feeding into **slow** forward-looking reasoning

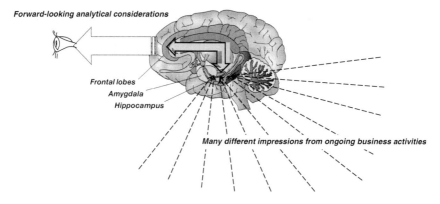

FIGURE 5.1 Interaction between fast and slow information-processing in the human brain.

monitoring of outcomes performed at regular intervals while considering the consequential outcomes multiple years ahead in time. This implies various interim learning loops where the corporate headquarters is updated about the realized outcomes in the local business entities that, when held against the intended corporate plans, can point to needed corrective actions and strategic initiatives for the near future. These strategic deliberations and related decisions can involve organizational members around top management at the corporate headquarters and may also involve line and local operational managers. This type of forward-looking strategic planning process is central as it is instigated by top management at the corporate center when they engage in forward-looking reasoning that underpins the formulation of strategic direction. Since these processes scrutinize many different aspects of the complex competitive environment and evaluate many alternatives, they constitute comprehensive time-consuming endeavors and consequently, they are *slow*.

A decentralized decision structure provides autonomy that allows local operational managers and employees to take responsive action within their areas of responsibility without asking for permission in advance. This delegates power and influence to organizational members in the local business entities that are closer to the relevant information and expertise needed to deal with unforeseen circumstances (e.g., Child and McGrath, 2001). Decentralization and delegation of power allows actions to be taken much faster in response to changing circumstances, that is, they are *fast*, and with better outcomes because the local decision makers possess the relevant information to decide on the proper responses. The fast responsive actions taken locally generate experiential insights as the operating managers observe what seems to work and what doesn't and within a relatively short time period, as actions quickly show particular results or effects. So, the local decision makers will receive fairly immediate feedback from the various stakeholders affected by the fast responses including close colleagues, employee groups and various customers, suppliers, business partners, etc. The impressions derived from such feedback create a good sense of the changing business environment that would otherwise remain unknown and invisible to the planning process around top management, if it were not collected and presented in a structured manner. The decentralized experiential insights obtained by local managers from their fast responses can generate important and useful updated information about the current changes in the competitive environment and potential implications for the organization.

The experiential insights of frontline stakeholders such as managers, employees, suppliers and customers scattered across operational business units and local subsidiaries can be identified and collected systematically for inclusion in the slow forward-looking planning process at corporate headquarters (see Chapter 4). This constitutes a promising opportunity to obtain unique updated insights about many subtle developments that otherwise might go unnoticed with the eventual consequences being unnoted until much later. Hence, when top managers particularly in complex multinational corporations have a limited number of direct business encounters to provide direct experiences from local market contexts, the updating of the competitive situation can become highly skewed by reinforcing conceptual interpretations from past personal experiences that become outdated and even irrelevant as time goes by. This can provide a lush breeding ground for cognitive biases among executive decision makers as they distance themselves from the daily operational activities to circumvent information overload.

Therefore, it is essential to take account of the ongoing experiential learning obtained from the fast operational responses taken by subsidiary managers in the local markets across the multinational organization in response to regional market changes, and consider these insights in forward-looking corporate strategy-thinking to avoid being blindsided. The central planning processes at corporate headquarters should be informed by current experiences gathered from individuals operating at the local decentralized entities across different regional markets (see Chapter 1). This way the fast responses taken in the local markets can interact with the slow forward-looking strategic-thinking process at headquarters and vice versa. That is, when the slow planning process deliberates about expected future conditions it should be informed by current updated insights gathered from fast ongoing operational activities as a testing ground for business opportunities and solutions. This calls for strategic thinking at the center around the corporate headquarters that is connected to the responsive actions taken by local operating managers. The frontline staff members of the overseas subsidiaries work closely together with various stakeholders executing the day-to-day business transactions and thereby learn first-hand from their reactions to the ongoing events.

Central planning and local responses

The slow multinational planning process at corporate headquarters can develop a shared cognitive understanding of the global competitive environment by engaging key decision makers in the discussions and express sensible corporate mandates for the future actions of local subsidiaries (e.g., Ansoff, 1965). By engaging decision makers from different parts of the multinational corporation in the discussions it is possible to consider a much broader set of skills, knowledge, and experiential insights from local market contexts, thereby forming a more nuanced shared cognition of the global business environment. The multinational corporate planning process can be interpreted as a discourse to reconcile diverse views and shape a better, more truthful interpretation of the ongoing developments in the global environment as a basis for giving general guidance or strategic mandates to decision makers throughout the organization. The fast, decentralized decision-making processes that allow empowered local managers to respond and explore alternative solutions generate updated insights about local market conditions. The autonomous local responses allow dispersed experimentation as the only viable way to uncover and test alternative business opportunities under pervasive uncertainty and consider their potential in the central planning process at the corporate headquarters.

Some examples can illustrate how local autonomous decision-making processes can help multinational corporations become more responsive. China's business leaders are well known for controlling companies in strictly top-down-driven structures, but what is less well known is how much Chinese enterprises decentralize, because it helps them respond to market shifts and rapidly add new business lines. The need for adaption of business activities is constant in China. Adaptation involves keeping pace not just with the local market but also with differences in developments across each of the provinces and the power of local officials. Because such differences can be evident, Chinese companies have recently begun to create structures that give subsidiaries nearly total autonomy. Consider Midea, China's second-largest home appliances maker, based in Shunde, a city across the border from Hong Kong. Midea produces everything from vacuum cleaners and small water heaters to microwaves and air conditioners. The majority of the product lines operate as independent businesses rather than as parts of a larger matrixed organization. Each business unit has a leader responsible for its product lines, and has the authority to build a sales force, line up suppliers and retailers, and construct factories where the best economic incentives are present. The idea of synergies across units has been replaced as there is a focus on autonomy and accountability. Midea is just one of many Chinese companies that operate with decentralized market approaches (Hout and Michael, 2014).

Haier, China's leading home appliance maker, comprising thousands of minicompanies, as the world's fastest-growing provider of appliances may represent an extreme example. It has been recognized as one of the most innovative companies and figures among China's ten leading innovative companies. Haier's approach to innovation builds on allowing employees to self-organize. Haier has created a flat management structure that puts customer needs at the core of the product development process and drives the entrepreneurial innovation among employees. Staff is encouraged to track evolving market trends and form autonomous project teams to address and take advantage of emerging opportunities. Haier refers to these self-organizing employee working groups as *ZZJYT*, which is a Chinese acronym referring to 'independent operation unit'. Haier uses these independent units to create a unique talent pool with a bidding system that allows self-organizing business units to present and bid on project proposals and to vote out incompetent leaders (Fast Company Magazine, 2014).

The fast responsive actions taken in local operating entities can quickly exchange needed information and knowledge with other entities through IT-enhanced communication links between operational unit managers and managers in different overseas subsidiaries, to coordinate responsive actions informally through mutual adjustments (Galbraith, 1994). The management reporting and associated information exchanges can be supported by IT-enhanced communication links to facilitate dynamic interaction between slow planning at headquarters and fast action taken in the local business units. This ability to openly exchange information and knowledge among organizational members with different types of market insights, functional expertise, and corporate responsibilities is a precondition for innovative collaborative learning that thrives on diverse knowledge and insights.

The combined fast and slow processes across business units and management levels of the multinational corporation can stimulate an underlying *dynamic system* that constitutes the very mechanism that drives effective strategic responsiveness (Andersen et al., 2007). Hence, a combination of fast and slow processes can create a dynamic system suited to drive corporate business activities towards meaningful responsive actions and thoughtful corporate moves, redirecting business activities and adapting the strategy under uncertain and unpredictable conditions (e.g., Bettis and Hitt, 1995). The fast responsive actions taken in local overseas subsidiaries operate in conjunction with responsive actions taken in other parts of the multinational organization that, over time, together will uncover opportunities that provide a better fit with the emerging global business environment. That is, an ongoing corporate strategy-making process that combines slow forward-looking strategic thinking at headquarters with dispersed operational responses in the local subsidiaries can be construed as a dynamic adaptive system with response capabilities that produce favorable risk–return outcomes for the multinational corporation (see Box 5.1).

BOX 5.1 The risk–return effects of a multinational organization

A multinational organization can provide scale and scope advantages with access to different factor endowments and arbitrage opportunities that allows for optimization of international price differentials and activity shifts in view of changing economic conditions. A flexible operating structure can improve the ability to handle major economic exposures and access to diverse multi-national resources can facilitate corporate responsiveness where the ability to switch activities between multinational entities can take advantage of fluctu-ations' relative prices. A global presence gives access to diverse skills, com-petencies, and insights in different parts of the corporation and constitutes potential sources for entrepreneurial business development. This innovative capacity can drive innovative business ventures that expand the strategic op-tions and make more strategic alternatives available for the multinational cor-poration for increased maneuverability under environmental change.

Conversely, flexibility options have maintenance costs and managing an extended multinational organization carries with it incremental communica-tion and coordination costs. An extensive multinational business presence can lead to demanding management, coordination, and communication chal-lenges, enhanced by cultural and institutional differences across countries.

The empirical evidence suggests that a multinational organization has favorable performance and risk features where upside potential can be en-hanced and downside losses subdued. This indicates that a multinational network structure comprised of linked overseas business entities operating

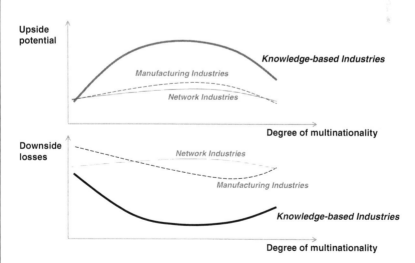

FIGURE 5.2 The knowledge-based risk–return effects of multinational enterprise.

across diverse national contexts can have corporate flexibilities based on diverse knowledge to develop responsive global opportunities for renewal. This ability is particularly associated with knowledge-based industries (Figure 5.2). However, the effects are not linear, i.e., the favorable risk-performance effects can be reached by operating across a handful of well-selected markets or regions whereas an extensive geographical reach has diminishing return effects. In more capital intensive network and manufacturing industries characterized by sizeable and irreversible investment in productive assets, the favorable outcomes of multinationality are not so pronounced (Andersen, 2012).

The favorable risk–return effects of the multinational organization derive from the combined ability to deflect downside loss events and to exploit the upside earnings potential of emerging business opportunities across multiple national market contexts. The effects are apparent among multinational organizations operating in different manufacturing and service sectors rather than a narrow subset of internationalized manufacturing companies (Andersen, 2011). The favorable risk–return effects go beyond conventional arguments of operational flexibilities, across a multinational structure where it is evident that multinational response capabilities are driven by knowledge-based flexibilities with access to diverse corporate resources.

This implies that a multinational organization should have leadership and management competencies to support the underlying adaptive mechanisms and engage in effective strategic renewal. This entails the formation of a multinational network structure comprised of many individuals residing both inside and outside the organization, tied together through open communication links (Figure 5.3). These network structures, such as the example of Haier, can be enabled by advanced communication and information technologies (CIT) and supported by an organizational culture and leadership traits that facilitate collaborative learning processes. This can exploit the collective intelligence contained among many diverse and engaged individuals across corporate functions and overseas subsidiaries located in different local and regional market contexts.

The multinational organization constitutes a complex corporate network structure with tight IT-enhanced communication links within individual business units, including overseas subsidiaries, between these diverse corporate entities, each of which have multiple communication links to external stakeholders. From an organizational perspective the internal communication links provide the means to exchange functional expertise and local market insights across various business entities to enable innovative development projects and engage in informal coordination of corporate activities. From an open network perspective the external communication links provide the means to access important business reconnaissance on new technologies, competitor moves and customer needs, while drawing on intimate relationship knowledge and community ties to forge relevant business development initiatives.

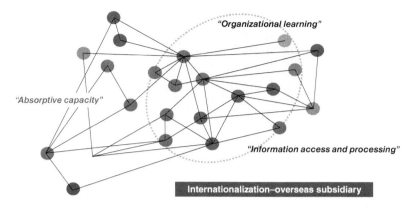

FIGURE 5.3 Communication links between internal and external network nodes.

Exploiting subsidiary knowledge

The overseas subsidiaries are located directly in the regional market contexts and provide the means to access unique resources bounded in local managerial and operating practices, locally adapted business offerings, and specific applications of modern technologies. The ability to utilize this diversity of knowledge-based resources will depend on the *control mechanisms* imposed by the corporate headquarters (e.g., Andersson, Forsgren and Holm, 2002; Andersson, Björkman and Forsgren, 2005). Multinational organizations that adopt direct control mechanisms imposed by centralized policies and restraining practices are less likely to exploit this resource opportunity compared to organizations that apply more general output controls that evaluate specific performance criteria in open discussions between local and headquarter management. A less restraining control approach will allow the potential advantages of the *local embeddedness* of overseas subsidiaries to come to fruition. The main advantages are ascribed to the innovative capacity of the multinational organization where the uniqueness of local business interactions can facilitate new *knowledge creation* that can be transferred across the corporate structure. Hence, other business units within the multinational corporate structure may be able to generate new offerings to the market and implement them through informal collaborative arrangements among disbursed managers with access to corporate resources in offerings that cater to local needs.

There are a number of necessary prerequisites for the ability to engage in innovative activities across the multinational corporation, including leadership and managerial capabilities, and a structure of interactive fast and slow decision-making processes with organizational slack and financial reserves to induce explorative behaviors. The multinational corporation provides incremental opportunities from the geographically dispersed business activities with differentiated local market insights that must be made available through a common ownership structure or linked by common core values promoted in self-organized COINs. The availability of sufficient organizational resources from financial slack can support creative behavior and development of multinational business opportunities with a subsequent potential to exploit their upside potential by executing project investments. This understanding has important implications for the way we perceive effective internationalization processes and potential performance effects derived from multinational enterprise.

The intensification of global competition increases the pressures for economic efficiencies from scale and scope economies and resonates with an increased focus on lean manufacturing and other means to reduce resource utilization in production processes (Apte and Goh, 2004; Womack and Jones, 2010). However, it is equally important for the multinational corporation to maintain a sufficient level of financial slack to induce innovative behaviors and advance the potential for global innovation. This is instrumental for achieving strategic responsiveness and with that the ability to adapt the multinational corporate strategy in the face of a constantly changing competitive landscape. Hence, it is necessary to strike a proper balance between strategic and operational integration to gain economic efficiencies and provide sufficient slack to extract the incremental benefits from future growth options that will drive the adaptive moves of the multinational corporation. This can only be accomplished with due consideration to proper corporate values, cultural features and an interactive organizational structure with IT-enhanced communication capabilities that link engaged individuals across the many multinational corporate business activities.

The integrative nature of the multinational strategy-making process illustrates that decision structure, communication and information-processing systems constitute important organizational features of a *dynamic adaptive system*. In turbulent global business environments organizations must be able to process a large amount of information across many constituents to form a meaningful updated understanding of the complex competitive environment involving a multiplicity of individual specialists with unique competences, knowledge and insight (Child and McGrath, 2001). Open communication channels can ensure that market observations, updated insights, and innovative ideas can be exchanged laterally across business units and brought forward to the slow planning system for analytical considerations in forward-looking strategic thinking. Hence, the multinational organization can conduct updated forward-looking strategic evaluations of the business opportunities uncovered by ongoing experiences from decentralized actions taken in business units and overseas subsidiaries. The open communication across different business entities and up and down management levels in the corporate hierarchy can provide a basis for collaborative learning among many diverse individuals.

Collaborative learning

Creativity and innovation are important evolving properties derived from the interacting fast and slow processes where human cognition about the competitive reality is formed through combined processes of reasoning and ongoing actions. New innovative ideas and business propositions can arise in both processes, although the eventual judgment about which ideas and propositions are better for the multinational corporation derives from the slow forward-looking process of reasoning. The central planning processes at headquarters consider alternative strategic directions through analytical reasoning where future consequences are assessed in simulated analyses based on basic assumptions about the environment. When the strategic mandates from the corporate headquarters are carried out in different business entities and subsidiaries around the world, the local managers take fast, decentralized action to execute business activities in line with the intent of the central headquarters mandate. However, they may also take autonomous responsive action in consideration of emerging changes that contradict the initial environmental assumptions, some of which might be unique to the local market context. The intuitive sensing of the effects experienced from local responsive actions constitutes a central element of the fast processes in the multinational corporation. The new experiential insights gained from local responsive actions taken in the fast system can be collected and passed on to the slow reasoning system at headquarters for further systematic analytical consideration in the forward-looking strategic planning process. This constitutes the interaction between fast responsive local actions in dispersed subsidiaries and the slow forward-looking strategic reasoning at corporate headquarters.

McKinsey & Company is a global market leader in strategy consulting and proponent of the interactive form of knowledge management as a means to advance a collaborative learning environment. The company emphasizes the professional responsibility of each employee to contribute knowledge transfer across the company's international business entities. It has recognized collaboration as a group norm where the employees' contribution to the collaborative knowledge transfer is part of the personnel evaluation process. One of the tasks at McKinsey is to prepare a summary of how and what each individual has learned from a completed project. This document is uploaded to an enterprise system, referred to as the "Practices Development Network," for broader sharing with co-workers. This system also includes a "Knowledge Resource Directory" as a guide to who knows what, and who has done what kind of projects with the company. An employee can find a list of experts by tapping into this database, and reach out to the people with relevant subject expertise. McKinsey's knowledge management system encourages employees to learn and teach collaboratively, which enhances the transfer of knowledge and the ability to adapt and compete over time (Lee and Jin, 2014).

Similarly, Mercy Corps, an international relief and development organization, promotes collaboration between employees worldwide advancing the desire to learn by establishing an informed learning network in organization-wide, technology-supported virtual communities of practice. The employees are encouraged to allocate 5 percent of their work time on learning and these activities are included in their job descriptions. By integrating learning as part of the job, Mercy Corps highlights the organizational commitment to learning. Executive-level cross-agency discussions are organized twice a year to encourage collaboration among agencies and support communities of practice and virtual teamwork at all levels. Mercy Corps has introduced an online collaboration platform, Clearspace, where employees can communicate their learning experiences (Lee and Yin, 2014).

So, individual employees and local operational managers do not act in a vacuum but operate as social organizational beings, executing the daily transactions in pursuit of a common purpose in accordance with a general strategic mandate from headquarters. The dispersed autonomous decision makers can inform and coordinate their actions through horizontally networked communication links while receiving feedback from various affected stakeholders. This provides the insights to make sense of the evolving business situations and their effect on the surrounding business environment. Hence, the ability of individual decision makers to take responsive action under changing conditions is important for gaining updated environmental insights and thereby generating viable solutions for ongoing strategic adaptation in the multinational corporation.

The ability to adapt to complex unpredictable situations under uncertain conditions requires collaborative efforts, drawing on insights from many diverse individuals. The cognitive capacity of humans is limited where the amount of information required to handle highly complex and ambiguous circumstances exceeds the capacity of even the smartest and most intelligent individual (Antonenko et al., 2010). Ambiguous and uncertain situations require involvement of different types of knowledge, expertise and insights to generate alternative ideas for viable solutions, which makes collaborative learning processes among multiple individuals more effective. Hence, the human cognitive limitations can be circumvented by engaging many individuals located in different market contexts in the collaborative learning process drawing on their diverse knowledge and environmental insights (Kirschner et al., 2009). This can be made a part of the complementary interaction between the insights gained from fast responses taken in local markets and the slow, forward-looking analytical reasoning in the planning process at corporate headquarters.

Interactive multinational management

The management and international business literatures tell us little about how the interactive fast and slow strategy-making processes should be organized to form a dynamic adaptive system and there has only been limited attention given to the role of management controls in this context (Simons, 1994). The control process implied by the conventional strategic management approach is a simple, long-looped diagnostic ex post comparison between intended and realized outcomes reviewed at the end of each planning cycle. There has been a substantial following for more elaborate balanced scorecards with quarterly or monthly follow-up interventions (e.g., Kaplan and Norton, 2001). The strategy field has acknowledged a need for ongoing monitoring of strategic performance, particularly in turbulent global business environments (e.g., Ansoff, 1980). However, there are significant challenges associated with these environmental conditions because there is general uncertainty about the real competitive outcome effects of chosen strategies as well as major uncertainties associated with the ability to carry out planned strategic initiatives (Goold and Quinn, 1990).

This is where the collective intelligence of many involved individuals may be helpful, because they represent an ability to assess what works for the multinational organization and better understand the evolving competitive environment in a complex global context. It also speaks to the potential of collaborative learning, finding viable solutions to complex issues by engaging the collective intelligence among many diverse individuals with different functional, business and geographical insights. This obviously can be tied together in the interactive fast and slow processes of local responsive actions, and central forward-looking reasoning at headquarters, as a way to form a dynamic adaptive system.

The collaborative learning processes outlined in cognitive science can be a strong basis for creative thinking and the development of innovative solutions to complex strategic issues challenged by the ambiguous, uncertain and unpredictable nature of the global business environment. The multinational network structure has the potential to link many people, in different parts of the organization, with outside stakeholders in open networks enabled by communication and information technologies (CIT) that can facilitate collaborative learning and exploit the collective intelligence of the diverse individuals.

From the perspective of the overseas subsidiary situated in the local business environment, such communication networks provide the means to engage in internal collaborative learning processes by enabling the free exchange of ideas, knowledge, and diverse insights among organizational members (Figure 5.4). The communication links to external stakeholders in the local market provide access to the processing of relevant environmental information from important sources outside the confines of the organization. It can also provide insights about competitor and partner conduct as a source inspiration for new or different ways of conducting the business activities provided the subsidiary has the *absorptive capacity* to learn from it and impose it on the organization.

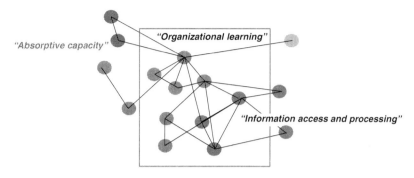

FIGURE 5.4 The internal and external communication links of a local subsidiary.

While this basic thinking can be applied to the context of the single local subsidiary, the implied network perspective is obviously much broader when considered in a global context. The broader geographical reach of a multinational corporation, with multiple overseas subsidiaries embedded in different local market contexts with their own local network connections, paints a picture of a vastly extended network of both internal agents located in different subsidiaries but also external agents in many different market contexts (Figure 5.5). When the individual subsidiary networks are combined across the full geographical reach of the multinational organization it constitutes a much wider and more richly connected network of diverse but also deep local market insights.

By extension, this implies that the learning and value creation potential across a broader, more diverse set of interlinked subsidiaries is extended accordingly, provided the implied coordination costs do not become excessive. In other words, the multinational network structure has potential advantages as an enhancer of knowledge-based business development through more extended collaborative learning processes across a diverse mix of individual expertise and insights. The formation of multinational network structures often takes place in the form of transitional phases enacted over time as management pursues and responds to emerging opportunities following an evolutionary process rather than a deliberate plan (Malknight, 1996). While the location of specific business activities in particularly advantageous regions may carry benefits by itself, there could also be incremental multinational benefits associated with enhanced innovative endeavors and the development of business opportunities. There has indeed been a gradual transition towards the creation of multinational networked structures, influenced by economic interdependencies between the national market contexts and shifts towards competing in cross-border product markets.

The dispersion of decision-making power to pursue operational and strategic autonomous actions in the local subsidiaries allows exploratory

The communication links of the overseas subsidiary

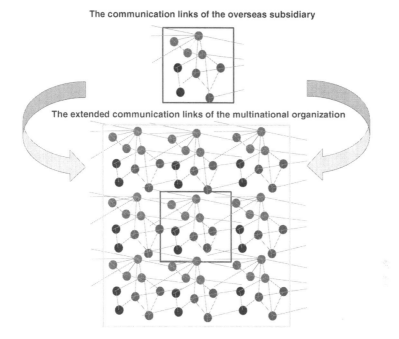

The extended communication links of the multinational organization

FIGURE 5.5   A networked multinational organization of overseas subsidiaries.

initiatives to be instigated by local operating managers that may uncover new global business opportunities. The strategic management process at corporate headquarters, with its related control systems, can be used for forward-looking assessments of the strategic opportunities uncovered by decentralized experimental actions. The management information systems can be used to channel new insights and can serve as vehicles for engaging in interactive discussions between top management at headquarters and local subsidiary managers to create a new and better understanding. Hence, the ability to integrate dispersed strategic responses and central reasoning in forward-looking planning can provide a dynamic to improve the interpretation of the changing business conditions and develop viable adaptive solutions inspired by the updated insights from the dispersed responses.

This can be supported by high-frequency monitoring, communication and collaborative learning processes that tie the fast–slow processing system together. The multinational corporation must find a proper balance between periodic management reporting, interactive control meetings, and informal communication approaches where updated information and knowledge is exchanged informally. This structural formula must be tailored to the firm-specific needs and conditions of the multinational corporation, promising to become a key to sustainable performance based on unique strategic response capabilities that are hard to emulate.

Summary

The combination of autonomous responses at local business entities and forward-looking planning at central headquarters forms a dynamic system of fast and slow processes in the multinational corporation, facilitated by communication and information technology linking diverse individuals across the global network. The ability to utilize local subsidiary entrepreneurial knowledge and insights in line with the strategic mandate outlined at headquarters creates a dynamic adaptive system that finds new viable ways to conduct business from decentralized experimentation guided by central intent.

References

Andersen, T. J. (2011). The risk implications of multinational enterprise. *International Journal of Organizational Analysis*, **19**(1): 49–70.
Andersen, T. J. (2012). Multinational risk and performance outcomes. *International Business Review*, **21**(2): 139–152.
Andersen, T. J. and Fredens, K. (2013). The Responsive Organization. CGSR Working Paper Series, No. 1. Copenhagen Business School, Denmark.
Andersen, T. J., Denrell, J. and Bettis, R. A. (2007). Strategic responsiveness and Bowman's risk–return paradox. *Strategic Management Journal*, **28**(4): 407–429.
Andersson, U., Björkman, I. and Forsgren, M. (2005). Managing subsidiary knowledge creation: The effect of control mechanisms on subsidiary local embeddedness, *International Business Review*, **14**: 521–538.
Andersson, U., Forsgren, M. and Holm, U. (2002). The strategic impact of external networks: Subsidiary performance and competence development in the multinational corporation. *Strategic Management Journal*, **23**: 979–996.
Ansoff, H. I. (1965). *Corporate Strategy: Business Policy for Growth and Expansion.* London, UK: McGraw-Hill.
Ansoff, H. I. (1980). Strategic issue management. *Strategic Management Journal*, **1**(2): 131–148.
Antonenko, P., Paas, F., Grabner, R. and van Gog, T. (2010). Using electroencephalography to measure cognitive load. *Educational Psychology Review*, **22**(4): 425–438.
Apte, U. M. and Goh, C. H. (2004). Applying lean manufacturing principles to information intensive services. *International Journal of Services Technology and Management*, **5**(5–6): 488–506.
Bettis, R. A. and Hitt, M. A. (1995). The new competitive landscape. *Strategic Management Journal*, **16**(S1): 7–19.
Black, J. S. and Gregersen, H. B. (2000). High Impact Training: Forging Leaders for the Global Frontier. *Human Resource Management*, **39**(2, 3): 173–184.
Child, J. and McGrath, R. G. (2001). Organizations unfettered: Organizational form in an information-intensive economy. *Academy of Management Journal*, **44**(6): 1135–1148.
Cotton, J. L., Vollrath, D. A., Froggatt, K. L., Lengnick-Hall, M. L. and Jennings, K. R. (1988). Employee participation: Diverse forms and different outcomes. *Academy of Management Review*, **13**: 18–22.
Dachler, H. P. and Wilpert, B. (1978). Conceptual dimensions and boundaries of participation in organizations. *Administrative Science Quarterly*, **23**: 1–39.

Fast Company: The Top 10 Most Innovative Companies in China, February 10, 2014. Retrieved on June 25, 2016 from http://www.fastcompany.com/most-innovative-companies/2014/industry/china.

Galbraith, J. R. (1994). *Competing with Flexible Lateral Organizations*. Reading, MA: Addison-Wesley.

Goold, M. and Quinn, J. J. (1990). The paradox of strategic controls. *Strategic Management Journal*, **11**(1): 43–57.

Hayes, J. (2007). *The Theory and Practice of Change Management* (second edition). Hampshire, UK: Palgrave Macmillan.

Hout, T. and Michael, D. (2014). A Chinese Approach to Management. *Harvard Business Review*, September 2014.

Huy, Q. N. (2011). How middle managers' group-focus emotions and social identities influence strategy imple- mentation. *Strategic Management Journal*, **32**(13): 1387–1410.

Kaplan, R. S. and Norton, D. P. (2001). *The Strategy-Focused Organization: How Balanced Scorecard Companies Thrive in the New Business Environment*. Brighton, MA: Harvard Business Press.

Kirschner, F., Paas, F. and Kirschner, P. A. (2009). A cognitive load approach to collaborative learning: United brains for complex tasks. *Educational Psychology Review*, **21**(1): 31–42.

Lee, S. and Jin, Y. (2014). How can companies harness a learning organization to lead the collaborative culture? Retrieved on June 25, 2016 from Cornell University, ILR School site http://digitalcommons.ilr.cornell.edu/.

Locke, E. A., and Schweiger, D. M. (1979). Participation in decision-making: One more look. In B. M. Staw (ed.) *Research in Organizational Behavior* (vol. 1, pp. 265–339).

Malknight, T. (1996). The transition from decentralized to network-based MNC structures, *Journal of International Business Studies*, **27**(1): 43–65.

March, J. G. (1991). Exploration and exploitation in organizational learning. *Organization Science*, **2**(1): 71–87.

Miller, K. I., and Monge, P. R. (1986). Participation, satisfaction, and productivity: A meta-analytic review. *Academy of Management Journal*, **29**(4): 727–753.

Mintzberg, H. and Waters, J. A. (1985). Of strategies, deliberate and emergent. *Strategic Management Journal*, **6**(3): 257–272.

Reeves, C., Love, P. and Tillmanns, P. (2012). Your strategy needs a strategy. *Harvard Business Review*, September, 2012.

Simons, R. (1994). How new top managers use control systems as levers of strategic renewal. *Strategic Management Journal*, **15**(3): 169–189.

Teece, D. J. (2007). Explicating dynamic capabilities: The nature and microfoundations of (sustainable) enterprise performance. *Strategic Management Journal*, **28**(13).

Teece, D. J. (2014). A dynamic capabilities-based entrepreneurial theory of the multinational enterprise. *Journal of International Business Studies*, **45**: 8–37.

Tsoukas, H. and Chia, R. (2002). On organizational becoming: Rethinking organizational change. *Organization Science*, **13**(5): 567–582.

Wagner, J. A. (1994). Participation's effects on performance and satisfaction: A reconsideration of research evidence. *Academy of Management Review*, **19**(2): 312–330.

Whitley, R. (2003). Changing transnational institutions and the management of international business transactions. In by Djelic, M. L. and Quack, S. (Eds.) *Globalization and Institutions: Redefining the Rules of the Economic Game*. Cheltenham, UK: Edward Elgar Publishing.

Womack, J. P. and Jones, D. T. (2010). *Lean Thinking: Banish Waste and Create Wealth in Your Corporation*. New York, NY: Simon and Schuster.

6

INTEGRATING LOCAL EXPLORATORY RESPONSES

Key points

- Innovation and business development
- Interactive multinational strategy-making
- Developing and executing global strategic options
- Multinational integration-responsiveness mechanisms
- Proactive risk-taking and adaptive learning

In this chapter we will further discuss the innovation and business development potential offered by a diverse multinational market presence across a multinational corporation, and consider the implications for opportunity capture to gain the upside performance potential. The chapter further explains how corporate decision makers at headquarters can integrate information obtained from dispersed initiatives in overseas subsidiaries to form a global adaptive dynamic.

It is commonly agreed that innovation and entrepreneurship behavior in the multinational corporation is essential for the ability to identify business opportunities and develop winning solutions that can renew the corporate business activities and adapt the firm to global environmental changes. Yet, rational analytical thinking and central integrative processing structures are also important for operating and executing business activities efficiently across a large multinational organization with a diverse local market presence (e.g., Brews and Hunt, 1999; Brown and Eisenhardt, 1997). The ability to adapt corporate business activities in the multinational organization does not really depend so much on the grand visions of top executives but is rather associated with a dynamic adaptive structure that can accommodate explorative initiatives in overseas business entities. The dual process concerns comprise fast responses across reasonably autonomous subsidiaries and central reflective thinking at the corporate headquarters honoring the conjoint needs for optimization and exploration in effective adaptive systems (e.g., Pfeifer and Bongard, 2007; Sutton and Barto, 1998). We have discussed these joint optimization and exploration phenomena as variations of intended and emergent strategies (Mintzberg and Waters, 1985), induced and autonomous strategy processes (Burgelman and Grove, 1996, 2007), and central versus decentralized strategy-making (Andersen, 2004; Andersen and Nielsen, 2009). Burgelman and Grove (2007) analyze how the combined induced and autonomous strategy processes should balance the corporate resource allocation between integrative central decisions by top management and dispersed exploratory decisions by local managers. This balancing act serves to ensure long-term strategic focus and economic rationality as well as the ability to develop new strategic business opportunities in time to implement fully when the competitive business environment changes in fundamental ways that may urgently challenge the competitive advantages of incumbent firms.

The adaptation and strategic renewal process in the multinational corporation has been conceptualized as dynamic capabilities (see Chapter 4) generally expressed as the organization's ability to sense environmental changes, seize new opportunities, and reconfigure the business activities to fit the changed competitive context (Figure 6.1) (Teece et al., 1997; Teece, 2007). The presence of dynamic capabilities can be ascribed to the specific knowledge and creative influence of many often specialized actors located in different parts of the organization.

A focus on dynamic managerial capabilities of top executives introduces the idea that heterogeneous cognitive capabilities of the executives in competing firms determine whether the organizations they lead are significantly better at adapting (Adner and Helfat, 2003). According to this logic the important resource committing decisions made by managers throughout the organization will influence the quality of the sensing, seizing and reconfiguration carried out as new strategic trajectories play out. This view suggests that those at the executive echelons carry out all the important decisions and constitute the prime actors in the strategic change process. However, the complex strategy-making process in large multinational corporations involves an amalgam of both central and dispersed decision makers that extend the cognitive perspective across many individual actors in the organization. Hence, the ability of executives to invoke dynamic capabilities will probably, to a larger extent, require cognitive leadership with the general

FIGURE 6.1 The three process elements of dynamic capabilities.

understanding that effective adaptive strategic renewal involves a combination of central and peripheral process elements.

The establishment of a responsive dynamic in the multinational corporation is commensurate with the conceptualization of *dynamic capabilities* conceived as the "ability to sense emerging changes in the local environments, seize new opportunities, and reconfigure the organization to exploit new opportunities offered by the changing competitive context" (Teece, 2007). The basic accomplishments of dynamic capabilities require an ability to obtain updated competitive intelligence, engage in entrepreneurial organizational behavior, some degree of autonomy, collaborative learning efforts, and structural flexibility to enable changes in the business activities. All of this resonates with the conditions that circumscribe the dynamic adaptive system in the multinational corporation. In a multinational context dynamic capabilities pay more attention to the role of dynamics, collaborative learning, and the augmentation of effective response capabilities, emphasizing the creation and co-specialization of new business activities and product markets based on entrepreneurial actions (Teece, 2014). Hence, the dynamic capabilities of the multinational corporation in essence build on interaction between fast and slow strategy-making processes, collaborative learning and flexibility to transform.

Although, the concept of dynamics capabilities has been part of the management vocabulary for more than a decade, it is relatively new in the practice of international business. The emerging technological capabilities have enabled firms to put dynamic capabilities into practice, for example, by facilitating online information exchange and communication between corporate agents and end-users fostering new types of collaboration in innovation. Multinational corporations use IT platforms for company-to-user interaction to sense product changes and distribute software applications and digital products such as music and games to their social, professional and consumer networks. Apple is an example of this. Apple wanted to legitimize the global sale of music online and worked to seize the opportunities of the Internet to use that mode of downloading music. The company convinced the record companies to collaborate and sell music together digitally (Shuen and Sieber, 2009). This illustrates how Apple used its sensing of the changing music distribution industry to seize opportunities for downloading music and reconfigure business activities to meet these changes ahead of competitors.

The dynamic view of the formal strategy-making process of the multinational corporation is formed by ex ante analyses of global competitive conditions, strategic alternative generation, choice of an optimal strategic path, outline strategic actions to realize stated objectives and monitor the ex post outcomes from the execution of planned actions. The subsequent monitoring and strategic control process can facilitate the updating of information and learning about changing competitive conditions, with suggestions for corrective actions and updated action plans (Goold and Quinn, 1990; Simons, 1990, 1994). When environmental conditions change frequently, abruptly, and in unexpected ways the dynamic updating elements of the strategy-making process become the most important factors, thereby embracing an emergent strategy perspective (Mintzberg and Waters, 1985).

The multinational decision structure and the supportive management information and communication systems become highly important features of an organization framework that can support dynamic adaptive strategy-making. In highly dynamic and complex global business environments the multinational corporation must be able to process increasing amounts of information that often resides with a multiplicity of individuals in different geographical locations with unique knowledge-based competencies (Child and McGrath, 2001). The formal solution for dealing with these demanding conditions is to move the decision-making rights down the organizational hierarchy, so the local operational entities where the individual expertise is located can make the decisions. Hence, we observe that the decision structure becomes more decentralized under environmental uncertainty although effective multinational corporations structure their business activities around central integrative processes (e.g., Child, 1997; Hill et al., 2000).

Decentralized decision-making increases the ability to respond to changing conditions in the local markets but is not sufficient to generate sustainable performance outcomes because this also requires that the dispersed multinational actions be integrated within an efficient global operational setup. Hence, the true challenge to dynamic adaptation is to combine central strategic thinking at corporate headquarters with decentralized responsive business experiments initiated by autonomous local managers and make them interact over time. Here the information-processing capabilities of the multinational corporation become essential because they can facilitate informal coordination between autonomous business entities across geographies and time zones, and exchange updated information between the periphery and the center (Galbraith, 1977, 1994). This can also comprise formal multipurpose management information systems that provide access to detailed performance information for top managers at corporate headquarters, as well as functional managers in local business units, to support open interactive discussions (Simons, 1994, 1995).

Interactive multinational strategy-making

Various studies have demonstrated the significance of autonomous decisions by local managers as important sources for building corporate competencies and developing overseas business opportunities that can turn into important strategic options for the multinational corporation (see Chapter 5). This depicts a strategy-making process that business development derives from local managers dispersed throughout the multinational organization as they take initiatives and respond to emerging competitive conditions. Here the prime responsibility of top management at corporate headquarters is to form an organizational structure that can support the ability to take autonomous initiatives and advance successful multinational business opportunities. The autonomous initiatives taken by local subsidiaries overseas then constitute the very source for the creation of multinational strategic options that subsequently can be executed successfully to become a part of the future corporate strategy (Figure 6.2).

Effective value enhancement from multinational strategic options hinges on the ability to create options at low cost and exercise the options optimally based on a superior understanding of the competitive context. The costless development of the strategic option builds on the entrepreneurial capabilities of managers and employees throughout the multinational corporation, as well as the organizational conditions for learning and innovation. The decisions to invest in strategic options and execute the underlying business opportunities must be informed by a broad network of individuals with diverse local market insights that can guide the exercise decisions in a flexible multinational operational structure that allows for the possibility of reorganizing corporate business activities. Hence, the multinational corporation will depend on effective communication between local business entities, functional specialists, and management at headquarters to identify strategic inflection points and choose among alternative multinational strategic options (Burgelman and Grove, 1996, 2007).

Here it is important that top management at headquarters and the corporate executive in general retain an open mind to new multinational ventures, with positive receptiveness to new multinational business propositions, no matter where they originate. A study of managers working for companies like AT&T, ConocoPhillips, Exxon Mobil and Walmart found that corporate leaders often rejected the innovation ideas they received from colleagues located in more distant geographical locations, because new ideas tend to threaten the existing power structures (Washburn and Hunsaker, 2011). Some multinational companies engage so-called bridgers to prevent idea options from distant subsidiaries being shot down. Omar Ishrak was the head of GE's medical

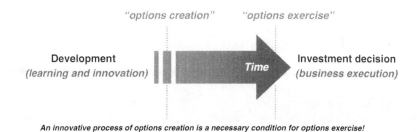

An innovative process of options creation is a necessary condition for options exercise!

FIGURE 6.2 The creation and exercise of multinational strategic options.

ultrasound division and acted as a bridger, helping some employees develop their business idea for portable ultrasound technology. He made sure that their efforts were integrated in GE by forming a new ultrasound division specifically for China, and giving them the autonomy needed to develop the product for that market. This created a smaller, cheaper device that made profits in different overseas markets operated by GE Healthcare Systems. Bridgers like Ishrak can be critical to the success of multinational corporations when persuading corporate executives to create room for new promising innovations despite their origin (Washburn and Hunsaker, 2011).

The dispersion of decision-making power makes it possible for local managers to engage in local autonomous business initiatives and make faster responses to ongoing changes as exploratory initiatives that can test what may work, thereby uncovering multinational business opportunities with the potential for success. The strategic planning process at corporate headquarters, along with supportive management control systems, can be useful for the ability to conduct forward-looking evaluations of multinational business opportunities identified in different parts of the organization and also develop associated strategic options that can take advantage of those business ideas (Figure 6.3).

We can think of this as a multinational funneling process where many local responses and business opportunities from different market contexts are collected for systematic consideration and arranged in a staged structure where further investments can be abandoned if the options fail to deliver. It represents a conscious process of learning from the responsive actions taken in different overseas business entities to find out what may work as a structured process in order to take advantage of those initiatives that turn out to be effective (e.g., Andersen, 2000, 2006). This way of conceiving

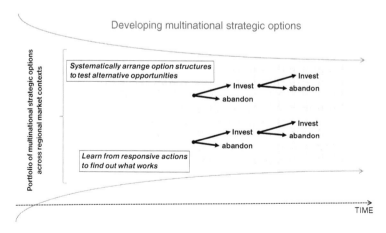

FIGURE 6.3 Arranging and learning from disbursed multinational strategic options.

strategy-making suggests that contemporary multinational organizations should adopt hybrid interactive structures that combine elements of intended central planning and emergence from autonomous initiatives taken by managers of geographically dispersed business entities. Hence, the outputs from central planning exercises may provide a platform that integrates various experiences of, and insights from, local subsidiaries as a basis for developing a common understanding of strategic conditions in the global business environment.

Strategic emergence in a multinational business context is driven by autonomous local initiatives, enabled by a decentralized decision structure, that allow managers in overseas subsidiaries to engage in responsive actions and experiment with new solutions to deal with the changing global environment. The local business unit managers operate within the confines of a strategic mandate from corporate headquarters and use IT-enhanced communication and information systems to coordinate activities with other business entities across the multinational organization (see Chapter 3). The ability to take local responsive actions at the overseas subsidiaries will encourage experimentation and thereby augment the chances of finding and developing successful multinational business opportunities that can deal effectively with changes in the business context. So, the multinational corporate strategy-making process should foster interaction between central planning at headquarters and autonomous strategic responses at local dispersed business entities, where management information and communication systems enable internal controls and open exchange of relevant information and knowledge.

The fast–slow dynamic in multinational strategy-making

Multinational corporations that are able to combine fast decentralized emergent strategy-making initiatives taken at the overseas subsidiaries with slow central strategic planning at the corporate headquarters are consistently found to be associated with superior economic performance (Andersen, 2004, 2013). The favorable performance outcomes can be explained by the effectiveness of an underlying dynamic system made up of the ability to take immediate local actions in response to ongoing changes and central forward-looking considerations that guide these responsive actions. The ongoing interactions and close proximity to the various stakeholders affected by the local initiatives can provide direct reconnaissance about what works and why as a basis for deeper understanding to inform corporate adaptive initiatives. The responsive actions taken at the overseas subsidiaries are carried out in line with the strategic mandate provided by the corporate headquarters as an essential output from a central planning process that, in turn, considers the updated information obtained from the overseas subsidiaries, reflecting their experiences with various decentralized actions.

The decentralized emergent strategy in the multinational corporation derives from local initiatives coordinated through the ongoing social interaction between networked individuals at dispersed overseas business entities and corporate headquarters. The dynamic interactive nature of these cross-border communication and information exchange processes makes the outcomes emergent, *nonlinear* and fairly unpredictable. The central planning process conducted at corporate headquarters considers updated information from the field and involves (many) individuals in structured forward-looking thinking about strategic alternatives assessed by rational analytical deductions and *linear* computations, with the aim of creating predictability and certainty. The interaction between the two fast and slow strategy-making processes provides an essential contrast between *nonlinear* and *linear* processes that are brought together as complementary elements in a *dynamic system* with highly adaptive properties in uncertain and unpredictable global market contexts.

As is the case with human cognition, the dynamic comprehension of evolving surroundings combines *fast* processes of actions and reactions and *slow* processes of forward-looking reasoning to determine what is happening, the consequences of it, and the proper ways to deal with the turbulent evolving environment (Andersen and Fredens, 2013). When unexpected events happen in the surroundings, they are noted and immediate responses are taken to fend off or exploit the given situation or set of circumstances. The short-term responses will have some effects and there will be reactions to them that are observed as new, fast insights obtained within a relatively short cycle-time (Figure 6.4).

The many multinational observations linked to the fast overseas responses against the changing local surroundings and the immediate

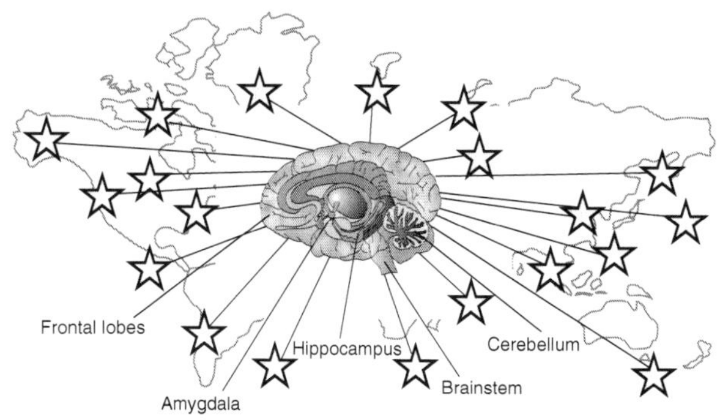

Unexpected events happen around the world

Responsive actions are taken in overseas subsidiaries – reactions observed locally → new fast insights!

FIGURE 6.4 The fast multinational response process as a source of new insights.

reactions incurred from them in the local markets provide a basis for observing general effects and thereby create fast local insights into changing market conditions (Figure 6.5). In human cognition central parts of the brain (the *amygdala* and *hippocampus*) channel all the impressions from the external environment to the *frontal lobes* for inclusion in slow forward-looking analytical considerations (unique to the human species) as a basis for interpreting the situations and determining a sensible way to move forward under the given circumstances.

We apply the principles of this fast–slow processing system in human cognition to better understand the many interactions that take place all the time among many individuals located in different parts of a multinational corporation across different geographical locations, functions and hierarchical management levels (see Chapter 5). The frontline employees and local managers execute the daily transactions of the overseas subsidiary that operate in their specific market contexts and they observe the environment from first-hand experiences to immediate responses and the way key stakeholders react to them. This multitude of impressions can either be collected and communicated systematically, or exchanged informally, up and down the hierarchy, so the local insights gained from fast responses can be made available to top management at corporate headquarters for their slow, forward-looking deliberations as important updates to their current understanding of the global competitive environment. Gaining access to current and updated insights from the local markets provides a basis for adapting the corporate strategic direction accordingly. This dynamic, which combines central planning at corporate headquarters with decentralized responsive

Responding to emerging changes in the global business environment

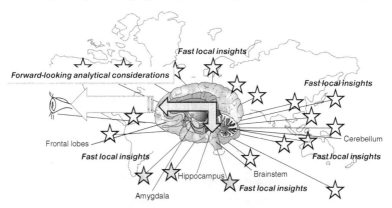

Combining *fast* local responses and observations with *slow* forward-looking reasoning at headquarters!

FIGURE 6.5   The slow reasoning process at headquarters to determine a way forward.

actions taken at local overseas subsidiaries, represents a multinational extension of the *interactive strategy-making* process (Andersen, 2004, 2013).

The combination of fast and slow processes can stimulate a *dynamic adaptive system* that de facto drives the ability of the multinational corporation to thoughtfully consider the dispersed responsive actions in the overseas subsidiaries and use the associated fast insights to adapt the multinational corporate strategy over time (see Box 6.1). This dynamic system facilitates immediate fast responsive action in the various local markets where the multinational corporation has a presence and at the same time uses these current experiences to update the understanding of the turbulent competitive environment and redirect corporate business activities towards thoughtful future activities that apply better to the evolving global business conditions (Andersen and Fredens, 2013). Hence, the combined fast–slow processing system makes sense of the changing surroundings and gives meaning and purpose to the forward-looking strategic considerations.

BOX 6.1 Different integration-responsiveness mechanisms observed in multinational corporations

The networked multinational corporations with multiple locations around the world, structured around a web of different operational functions and business activities, is highly complex and it is not obvious how to conduct the exchange of information and knowledge required to make the fast–slow processing dynamic work. Much of the internal communication activities are carried out in highly informal ways, supporting autonomous initiatives and actions, to the extent that the multinational corporation has installed state-of-the-art communication and information technologies to facilitate world-wide interaction and heeds a culture of open collaborative learning practices. However, in addition to this the corporate leadership can think of other more formal approaches to ensure ongoing interactions between the managers in the corporate headquarters and the local business entities as well as across managers located in overseas subsidiaries with a focus on local market contexts. Based on extensive field studies among a good handful of multinational corporations, a number of integration-responsiveness mechanisms have been identified that, in different ways, serve to create an interactive exchange of strategic information between managers with different functional, geographical and corporate strategy perspectives.

Local market mechanisms

The corporation establishes special functional entities either within existing subsidiaries or as an outside function to develop product and service features that cater specifically to local market needs, possibly by extending local assembly facilities for deliveries in local markets. The local sales teams that cater to different parts of the national market geography, meet regularly to discuss business opportunities and support different sales initiatives. This can be extended to also include production and development engineers, to discuss the potential for new innovation adaptations in formally allocated innovation day meetings.

For example, Uber is a highly multinational but locally market-driven company. It was founded in 2009 by Garrett Camp and Travis Kalanick, as a start-up to address the problems in the taxi industry, using efficient smartphone applications. The technology connects the taxi drivers directly to the customers as app users. Starting in January 2010, Uber has expanded significantly to now operating in more than 75 countries. The internationalization strategy is based on local strategic partnerships utilizing domestic resources and market knowledge. Hence, Uber has partnered with Baidu in China, Times Internet in India, Sberbank in Russia, Golden Pay in Azerbaijan and AmericaMovil throughout Latin America. In some regions, Uber contracts with local taxi companies, car rentals and private drivers. In other countries, Uber engages only with companies. The local partner strategy is pursued to enable adaptation to local legislative requirements and regulations and to follow pricing that is geared to the local market conditions (Cavusgil et al., 2017).

Regional management mechanisms

The national market focus can be extended to comprise oversight across broader regions where the national markets operate under comparable conditions. This can be manifested in the establishment of regional product centers that consider ways to apply regional technologies and create responses that cater to local market opportunities. This may also comprise formal scouting teams set up to search for innovative opportunities across the regional markets. These efforts to further regional sales initiatives can cater to long-term needs uncovered and discussed in regular meetings where regional partner firms and key customers can participate and voice opinions.

For example, when Hennes & Mauritz (H&M), as a leading multinational clothing retailer specialized in fast fashion, opens a new store, the opening is followed by intense scrutiny of its closest global competitors, e.g., GAP and Zara to discern their immediate responses and interim moves. H&M has found that styles vary across different geographical regions within the individual countries. For instance in the US, management has focused on trendy fashions in their city stores and on more conservative items in their suburban mall stores. H&M has also discovered that some regional consumers appreciate a more inviting atmosphere in their stores, whereas clothing requirements are more modest in other regions (Cavusgill et al., 2017). Hence, they provide substantial leeway for local managers where the head office provides substantial guidance on global strategy and store managers localize their marketing tactics to their market needs. At individual stores, the local managers can adapt pricing, advertising, and product range to suit the regional market conditions. As a consequence, the firm, for example, offers smaller sizes in Asia and more conservative apparel in Islamic countries.

The regional presence can also be better integrated into the corporate structure by physically moving executives with particular functional responsibilities to regional headquarters located geographically away from corporate headquarters in the home country. It can also be accomplished by setting up regional board committees that assume specific responsibilities for corporate operations across a particular region.

Central corporate mechanisms

Specific units located at corporate headquarters, with the purpose of adapting products to different markets, can ensure that they work in close interaction with sales managers and production engineers in the local markets. This may be complemented with central facilities dedicated to innovation, and professional training incorporating all parts of the multinational organization including central product development teams that stand ready to travel abroad to liaise with local development agents.

Consider for example Ikea, the leading global retailer of furniture. Ikea has different headquarter locations such as in the Netherlands, Sweden and Belgium, but the responsibility for product development, purchasing and warehousing is located in Sweden. The corporate headquarters designs and develops Ikea's global branding and product line and collaborate with the external suppliers. The well-known Ikea catalogue is aligned with Ikea's cosmopolitan style and each store follows a centrally developed advertising strategy in which the catalogue and a catalogue app are the most important marketing tools (Cavusgill et al., 2017).

General network exchanges

Most large multinational corporations arrange regular meetings for country and regional managers, providing a forum for the exchange of ideas and insights from local markets and to engage in open discussions about the strategic direction of their international corporate activities. Such information can also be garnered from advanced leadership conferences and meetings where top management at corporate headquarters travel regularly to local markets and regions to listen to local experiences and insights as well as discuss ongoing strategy considerations.

For example, Unilever, the Anglo-Dutch multinational consumer goods company co-headquartered in Rotterdam and London implemented global business services (GBS) in late 2009 aimed at taking the complexity out of businesses' processes that fail to provide value to the consumers. The initiative referred to as Enterprise & Technology Solutions (ETS) ultimately fell within the finance, HR, IT, information management, real estate and facilities management and indirect procurement sectors. The initiative addressed about 40 separate service lines, including purchase to pay, record to report, recruitment, master data, and facilities services. Unilever wanted to make each of these service-line operations simpler, cheaper and better. The company used to operate more than 400 intranets, one for almost every country, product group, brand, and function, so communication was not aligned and managers and employees were often uncertain about where to find information and how to communicate. ETS instituted a single global intranet, accessible in more than 20 languages that helped create a fluid exchange platform for management information and communication. This system can also be replicated for external partners, so an end-to-end process can include the operations of Unilever's suppliers and might eventually include the customers as well (Visée, 2015).

Responding in different business environments

The global environmental context can typically be characterized by two major dimensions, referred to as *complexity*, that is, the interrelatedness between different business activities, and *dynamism*, that is, the frequency of change in the way business activities are carried out. A business environment with few interrelated activities and few changes over time is considered stable where most developments are known and fairly well described. It constitutes a *simple* context. A business environment with many interrelated activities constitutes a *complex* context and an environment where things change frequently is a *dynamic* context. If the business environment is characterized simultaneously by many interrelated activities and frequent changes, it constitutes a *turbulent* context, which is particularly demanding to deal with and operate in (Figure 6.6).

In simple contexts the circumstances are more or less known and can be projected into the future, which makes it possible to solve identified problems through linear reasoning and the application of computational optimal algorithms. Complex contexts need more extensive analyses to better understand

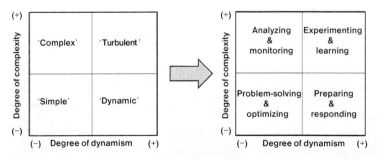

FIGURE 6.6 Global environmental conditions for proactive risk-taking and adaptive learning.

the underlying interdependencies and, in so doing, developing a more complete comprehension of the implied relationships that then can be monitored. In dynamic contexts things are changing all the time, often abruptly and in unexpected ways, which calls for preparedness and flexible structures to accommodate reorganizations to enable immediate responses. The turbulent contexts are the most demanding environments because dynamic changes in complex relationships make it impossible to predict the exact outcomes even if you understand the complex conditions (Andersen et al., 2014). Hence, the only way to deal with the inherent uncertainty and unpredictable nature of the environment is by experimenting through trial and error while learning from the various experiential insights collected from these endeavors.

This is exactly what is happening in the dynamic adaptive system constituted by the combined fast and slow processes of immediate local responses and ongoing forward-looking analyses of the environmental context at the center, considering the consequences of alternative strategic ways. In a multinational corporation the ability to exploit the diversity of knowledge and insights in order to identify new business opportunities and develop them into viable strategic options for further strategic consideration has favorable consequences for the risk–return profile displaying simultaneous positive effects on upside potential and negative loss effects (see Chapter 5). In others words, the enhanced innovative potential of multinational diversity and the built-in potential for operational flexibility can reduce the variability in realized earnings and cash flows, and increase net income. The advantage may relate to cheaper funding, more timely information, and an ability to act quickly, utilizing unique insights and knowledge, with access to diverse superior resources that enhance flexibility to change course by engaging in value-creating business opportunities.

The funding advantage arises because the reduced vulnerability of corporate earnings increases the debt service capacity and reduces the bankruptcy risk, so more funding is available at lower financial rates to finance positive business propositions (Froot et al., 1993). Lower cash flow volatility reduces the need to hold liquidity buffers in the form of excessive cash reserves that can release financial resources for investment in valuable business propositions promising economic returns well above the opportunity cost (Merton, 2005). Availability of better and more detailed information about competitive conditions derived from ongoing insights gained from responsive experiments can provide significant advantages where communication and information networks facilitate the ability to exploit this information among employees, customers, suppliers and partners. The engagement of local employees and managers and their ability to take autonomous responsive action provide a basis for testing alternative approaches and update the market intelligence for potential commercial use. The access to a unique intelligence platform with a supportive communication system allows organizational actors to better understand changing circumstances and engage in smarter, more effective adaptive moves.

For a multination corporation that constantly deals with uncertain conditions and moves forward in a global competitive environment that is largely unknown, at least in its future expressions, requires experimentation, learning and innovation to be effective and sustain performance through ongoing adaptation. This requires a risk-taking culture, but within a decentralized decision structure that allows autonomous initiatives in the local markets to test the viability of new business opportunities. The dispersed responsive initiatives taken in the local subsidiaries constitute low-risk probes in the sense that they do not expose the entire multinational corporation but can be tried out locally in a small scale and only advanced and developed further if they seem to work. Conversely, they can be skipped if they turn out not to work, at no extra cost to the multinational corporation. Hence, this is a significantly better approach than a centralized approach where top management at corporate headquarters may commit vast resources to a major global change process that will carry a substantial risk of failure, thereby jeopardizing the very existence of the entire organization. An interactive multinational strategy-making process, that combines fast local risk-probes with central forward-looking reasoning to consider further expansion of corporate level ventures, captures this very approach. The dynamic system created by fast actions and slow updated learning arguably resembles the approach behind the early success of Hewlett Packard where the company founders Bill Hewlett and Dave Packard are said to have a penchant for action and learning whereby they never studied a problem for long before taking action to implement a solution and, rather, learned from trying out things and adapting things along the way (House and Price, 2009).

The effective multinational corporation must engage in dispersed risk-taking behaviors where local agents can experiment and learn from their responsive initiatives. By decentralizing the decision structure, dispersed decisions in local market settings brings about a faster response to emerging events and gain updated experiential insights in trial-and-error learning from these responsive initiatives. The decentralized local initiatives constitute *low-risk probes* in the multinational corporation as opposed to *all-in stakes* committed at the corporate headquarters as a quick fix to match the current requirements across a multiplicity of overseas markets. At the same time corporate leadership must be receptive to the updated intelligence accessible from managers and employees in the local business entities.

Multinational corporations that have experienced prolonged success tend to ignore new updated knowledge and insights because it is in conflict with the *dominant logic* of the senior executives that forms their understanding of the global competitive environment based on their past successes (Bettis and Prahalad, 1995). That is, the successful experiences gained in the competitive environments of the past can be misleading for the emerging competitive contexts and therefore can create cognitive biases among senior decision makers. One way to circumvent these kinds of potential pitfalls is to form a culture of rebelliousness among people working in the organization, one that allows operating managers and employees to take their own initiatives within their decision-making powers (House and Price, 2009). There is often a tendency to emphasize business activities and competencies that underpin past success and continue to refine and optimize the way things are currently being carried out. But this creates problems when the competitive environment fundamentally changes and the past competencies become irrelevant, a conundrum often referred to as the *competency trap* (Levinthal and March, 1993). This also provides a partial explanation for the eventual demise of many former star performing global firms, as implied by the *Icarus syndrome* (Miller, 1990)[1].

In contrast to a corporation driven by the dominant logics of top management, a *mindful organization* consists of internal members that are cognizant of the many changes related to environmental and business intelligence, competitor intelligence and operational intelligence (see Chapter 4). These environmental conditions are observed by many local managers and frontline employees in their daily business encounters and constitute the weak signals that can predicate the emerging environmental events of strategic significance. The individuals that operate in many different parts of the multinational corporation can sense the subtle things that are evolving in the business environment before they happen. These observations, based on experiential insights, can be collected and communicated as highly useful updated information of potential strategic value for use in forward-planning consideration at corporate headquarters.

The ability to experiment throughout the organization, learn from those experiments, and use the generated insights in constructive innovation processes involving the diverse knowledge of many people around the world to generate promising business opportunities for the future, constitutes a form of dispersed risk-taking. The proactive risk-taking behavior is delegated to local subsidiary managers and people operating deep inside the multinational corporation. It represents a prudent way to gather new strategic reconnaissance among many diverse, knowledgeable, and engaged individuals and develop business opportunities and eventual strategic options with global staying power. This effectively builds the viable business propositions that respond effectively to the requirements of the future global business environment (Figure 6.7). Hence, ongoing experimentation dispersed across the multinational reach of the corporation creates the insights that are necessary to form an emerging understanding of the various operating elements that can shape the future multinational corporate business model. However, it is important that the corporate leadership shows openness and genuine willingness to consider the rich potential this distributed information has to update the current understanding of the competitive environment that circumscribes the existing business model.

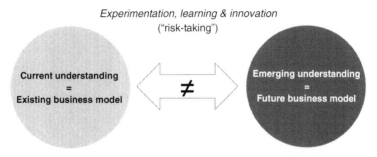

Experimentation, learning & innovation
("risk-taking")

Current understanding
=
Existing business model

≠

Emerging understanding
=
Future business model

FIGURE 6.7 Reducing the gap between the current and future multinational business model.

The insightful knowledge about global customer needs and the preferences held by local partners engaged in distribution, marketing and related services, are essential to building responsive business relationships for the future. Understanding the motivation and capabilities of potential entrants and providers of complementary products and services is important for foreseeing emerging events and responding to potential changes in the global competitive environment. The ability to respond quickly can provide an advantage vis-à-vis the competition. Fast responses, dependent on the pace of change in the specific industry, are supported by access to diverse information and knowledge, and form a good experiential basis for understanding the potential consequences of emerging developments. A rich and diverse set of updated experiences can be very useful when the organization is faced with surprising events because the diversity of experiential insights are the means to better interpret and comprehend what is happening as a basic prerequisite for developing proper solutions in a crisis situation. The experiential insights can be acquired from autonomous responses and ongoing learning from successes as well as mistakes. A multinational corporate setting that promotes collaborative learning and enhances knowledge exchange through communication and information systems will form a better organizational context for potential benefits to be harvested from the interactive multinational strategy-making process.

Summary

Innovation and entrepreneurship in the multinational corporation is essential for the development of new global business opportunities and grow from the sensing of regional market needs by individual managers disbursed across the local business entities. Strategic adaptation and renewal in the multinational corporation builds on the organization's ability to sense environmental changes, seize new opportunities, and reconfigure the multinational organization to fit the changing global competitive context. The effective integration of new local market opportunities can benefit from different integration-responsiveness mechanisms and a corporate culture of open collaborative learning from autonomous initiatives facilitated by communication and information systems across global business units.

Note

1 Icarus is known from the Greek mythology as the son of Daedalus, a master craftsman who construed the Labyrinth. Icarus attempted to escape Crete by flying with wings his father made from feathers and wax. But Icarus was warned about complacency and hubris to ensure that he neither flew too high close to the sun or too low next to the dampness of the sea. But alas, in excitement over own flight capabilities, Icarus ignored the advice and flew too close to the sun where the increasing heat causing the wax in his wings to melt so he eventually plunged into the sea. Miller (1990) uses this as a metaphor to describe the resemblance to the observed tendency of major successful corporations to sooner or later plunge into obliteration after years of success thereby displaying an *Icarus syndrome*.

References

Adner, R. and Helfat, C. E. (2003). Corporate effects and dynamic managerial capabilities. *Strategic Management Journal*, **24**(10): 1011–1025.

Andersen, T. J. (2000). Real options analysis in strategic decision making: An applied approach in a dual options framework. *Journal of Applied Management Studies*, **9**(2): 235–255.

Andersen, T. J. (2004). Integrating decentralized strategy making and strategic planning processes in dynamic environments. *Journal of Management Studies*, **41**(8): 1271–1299.

Andersen, T. J. (2006). Global Derivatives: A Strategic Risk Management Perspective. Harlow, UK: Pearson Education.

Andersen, T. J. (2013). *Short Introduction to Strategic Management*. Cambridge, UK: Cambridge University Press.

Andersen, T. J. and Fredens, K. (2013). The Responsive Organization. CGSR Working Paper Series, No. 1. Copenhagen Business School, Denmark.

Andersen, T. J. and Nielsen, B. B. (2009). Adaptive strategy making: The effects of emergent and intended strategy modes. *European Management Review*, **6**(2): 94–106.

Andersen, T. J., Garvey, M. and Roggi, O. (2014). *Managing Risk and Opportunity*. New York, NY: Oxford University Press.

Bettis, R. A. and Prahalad, C. K. (1995). The Dominant Logic: Retrospective and Extension. *Strategic Management Journal*, **16**(1): 5–14.

Brews, P. J. and Hunt, M. R. (1999). Learning to plan and planning to learn: Resolving the planning school/learning school debate. *Strategic Management Journal*, **20**: 889–913.

Brown, S. L. and Eisenhardt, K. M. (1997). The art of continuous change: Linking complexity theory and time-paced evolution in relentlessly shifting organizations. *Administrative Science Quarterly*, 1–34.

Burgelman, R. A. and Grove, A. S. (1996). Strategic dissonance. *California Management Review*, **38**(2): 8–28.

Burgelman, R. A. and Grove, A. S. (2007). Let chaos reign, then rein in chaos—repeatedly: Managing strategic dynamics for corporate longevity. *Strategic Management Journal*, **28**(10): 965–979.

Cavusgil, S. T., Knight, G. and Riesenberger, J. (2017). *International Business: The New Realities*. Fourth edition, Pearson Education Limited. Harlow, UK: Pearson Education.

Child, J. (1997). Strategic choice in the analysis of action, structure, organizations and environment: Retrospect and prospect. *Organization Studies*, **18**(1): 43–76.

Child, J. and McGrath, R. G. (2001). Organizations unfettered: Organizational form in an information-intensive economy. *Academy of Management Journal*, **44**(6): 1135–1148.

Froot, K. A., Scharfstein, D. S. and Stein, J. C. (1993). Risk Management: Coordinating Corporate Investment and Financing Policies. *Journal of Finance*, **48**: 1629–1658.

Galbraith, J. R. (1977). *Organization Design*. Addison Wesley Publishing Company.

Galbraith, J. R. (1994). *Competing with Flexible Lateral Organizations*. Reading, MA: Addison-Wesley.

Goold, M. and Quinn, J. J. (1990). The paradox of strategic controls. *Strategic Management Journal*, **11**(1): 43–57.

Hill, S., Martin, R. and Harris, M. (2000). Decentralization, Integration and the Post-Bureaucratic Organization: The Case of R&D. *Journal of Management Studies*, **37**(4): 563–586.

House, C. H. and Price, R. L. (2009). *The HP Phenomenon: Innovation and Business Transformation*. Stanford, CA: Stanford University Press.

Levinthal, A. D. and March, J. G. (1993). The myophia of learning. *Strategic Management Journal*, (Special Issue) **14**: 95–112.

Merton, R. C. (2005). You have more capital than you think. *Harvard Business Review*, **83**(11): 84–94.

Miller, D. (1990). *The Icarus Paradox: How Exceptional Companies Bring About Their Own Downfall*. New York, NY: Harper Business.

Mintzberg, H. and Waters, J. A. (1985). Of strategies, deliberate and emergent. *Strategic Management Journal*, **6**(3): 257–272.

Pfeifer, R. and Bongard, J. (2007). *How the Body Shapes the Way We Think: A New View of Intelligence*. Cambridge, MA: MIT Press.

Shuen, A. and Sieber, S. (2009). Collaborative innovation in action. Orchestrating the new dynamic capabilities. *Expert Insight*, Case: 1605–E., 58–65.

Simons, R. (1994). How new top managers use control systems as levers of strategic renewal. *Strategic Management Journal*, **15**(3): 169–189.

Simons, R. (1995). Control in an age of empowerment. *Harvard Business Review*, **73**(2): 80–88.

Sutton, R. S. and Barto, A. G. (1998). *Reinforcement Learning: An Introduction*. Cambridge, UK: MIT Press.

Teece, D. J. (2007). Explicating dynamic capabilities: the nature and micro-foundations of (sustainable) enterprise performance. *Strategic Management Journal*, **28**(13): 1319–1350.

Teece, D. J. (2014). A dynamic capabilities-based entrepreneurial theory of the multinational enterprise. *Journal of International Business Studies*, **45**(1): 8–37.

Teece, D. J., Pisano, G. and Shuen, A. (1997). Dynamic capabilities and strategic management. *Strategic Management Journal*, 509–533.

Visée, P. (2015). The global effective enterprise. *McKinsey Quarterly*, April 2015.

Washburn, N. T. and Hunsaker, B. T. (2011). Finding great ideas in emerging markets. *Harvard Business Review*, September: 3–9.

7

INTERACTIVE LEADERSHIP TO HARNESS LOCAL ENGAGEMENT

Key points

- The challenges of multinational corporate leadership
- The dynamic interaction between slow reasoning at headquarters and fast responses in subsidiaries
- Using coordination and cultivation to balance central and decentralized activities
- Interactive strategic resource management

This chapter discusses the leadership challenges associated with the interactive dynamic strategy-making process that encompasses traits that can furnish rational forward-looking analysis, dispersed decision-making power, broad autonomy, open discussions and collaborative learning as the key ingredients of the *responsive multinational corporation* (RMC). The effective corporate leader should give priority to frontline engagement with support for local field experiments and a willingness to learn from updated information and current experiential insights gained from across the many parts of the multinational organization.

The ability to gradually modify current business activities and adapt the corporate strategy to retain a proper fit with the changing requirements of the global competitive context remains the quintessential leadership challenge in contemporary multinational corporations (e.g., Agarwal and Helfat, 2009; Andersen et al., 2007; Burgelman, 1991; Chakravarthy, 1982; Crossan and Berdrow, 2003; McGrath, 2013; Simons, 1994). This ability will rely on the leader's capacity to foresee impending environmental changes, hone opportunities that can respond to these changes, and recombine accessible resources towards the execution of opportunity-driven strategic options. Managerial foresight and not least an openness to consider environmental changes sensed by actors operating deep within and around the organization are necessary prerequisites for effective strategic adaptation in a multinational context.

The multinational corporate leadership challenge is intricately linked to the interplay between top management at the corporate center and the engagement of locally dispersed managers and employees operating in overseas subsidiaries around the periphery of the organization. In this context the experiential insights of frontline employees and managers constitute essential updated information about current changes in the business environment with a sense for possible responses or solutions to deal with the new reality. It is important that the corporate leadership is able to facilitate the interactive strategy-making process that can incorporate updated information sensed by local managers operating in the periphery of the multinational organization and use these current insights in the forward-looking strategic reasoning performed at the corporate headquarters.

The experiential insights gained on an ongoing basis by local operational managers can be collected systematically for regular consideration of the slow strategic planning process conducted at the corporate center (see Chapter 4). This constitutes an opportunity to gain access to unique updated information about subtle environmental changes that otherwise are unavailable for top management (Andersen and Hallin, 2016). The failure to obtain updated insights will reinforce preconceived environmental perceptions based on prior experiences from an outdated environmental context. The resulting cognitive biases among executive decision makers can cause otherwise intelligent leaders to make less intelligent strategic decisions, with potentially fatal economic consequences (e.g., Bazerman and Moore, 2008).

Hence, it is essential for top managers to consciously account for the experiential learning that arises inside the organization from the many fast operational actions taken in response to immediate conditional changes in the many local task environments of the multinational corporation. That is, the central forward-looking planning considerations should be informed by updated experiences and insights obtained from the autonomous actions taken by managers in overseas business entities in response to changing conditions. The strategic thinking of top management must be connected to the responsive actions taken by employees and operational managers working in overseas subsidiaries in close proximity to the core stakeholders acting in those market contexts. The slow planning processes can in turn promote a shared cognitive understanding of the global competitive environment, engaging key people in the discussions as a basis for developing a generally accepted strategic direction for the corporation that can serve as a basis for the formulation of strategic mandates from headquarters to guide the local subsidiary activities. By involving key decision makers from many different parts of the multinational corporation the discussions will be exposed to a broader set of organizational constituents with different insights and experiences that may help form a more nuanced shared cognition about the current strategic situation in a global context.

When considering whether to decentralize particular decisions it is important to think about the implications of policy decisions and their influence on operational decision-making, that is, the interrelationship between decentralized and central decisions should be managed. For example, Cisco Systems manages its travel expense decisions through a combination of automated central policies and employee empowerment. This means that lower-level employees can make all their own travel arrangements without the approval of their managers as long as they make travel reservations on the Cisco intranet and charge all expenses with a special American Express card. Cisco operates with similar dual approaches for many other different types of expenses where the employees can decide for themselves when and what to buy as long as the expenses comply with centrally determined per diem guidelines and the system reimburses expenses without any management involvement at all (Malone, 2004).

The imposition of interactive processing approaches with more decentralized decision structures must embrace effective lateral (horizontal) and vertical communication channels that can tie together local operational managers, functional specialists and top managers in open information exchanges (e.g., Galbraith, 1994, 1995). These types of organizations are described as more decentralized, non-hierarchical and autonomous but also embrace central integrative processes and structures to engage in updated coordination and gain economic efficiencies. Decentralization increases the ability to take local responsive actions, but those actions must be taken with a view to the longer-term planning considerations to generate sustainable multinational performance outcomes. The open communication channels between individuals across operational functions, geographical locations, and hierarchical levels provides a basis for engaging in innovative collaborative learning among many diverse organizational members as a necessary prerequisite to develop more effective solutions addressing highly complex strategic issues.

The creative, innovative and entrepreneurial behaviors among individual employees and decision makers in the multinational corporation can arise as evolving properties from the conscious management of fast local responses and slow forward-looking planning considerations where cognition is formed through the ongoing interaction between reasoning and current updated insights from actions. New ideas and business opportunities can arise from both processes but the eventual judgment as to which business propositions are better for the long-term success of the multinational corporation derives from the slow forward-looking planning process at headquarters. The decentralized actions are taken locally in line with the intent expressed in the corporate strategic plan while, at the same time, responding to emerging changes in the local competitive environment. The ongoing intuitive observations made by the local stakeholders as they interpret the effects experienced from local responsive actions, derives from the fast system and can be passed on to the slow system associated with forward-looking planning at the center as updated environmental insights that can inform these considerations. This forms a dynamic adaptive system between fast actions responding to immediate changes in the competitive conditions inspired by the slow system where the ongoing observation of outcomes in the fast process are subsequently fed back into the slow process for forward consideration.

When dealing with complex strategic issues under uncertain and unpredictable conditions in the global business environment, top management can circumvent their cognitive limitations by activating many individuals across the multinational corporation with diverse knowledge and involving them in problem-solving through collaborative learning (Kirschner et al., 2009). This can be accomplished within the interactive strategy-making process, where diverse information is processed among many individuals from different parts of the organization, counting updated insights from fast responsive actions in local dispersed market contexts and the slow forward-looking corporate planning process. Hence, a collection of diverse knowledgeable and engaged individuals, including both central decision makers around top management at corporate headquarters and operational managers in local overseas subsidiaries, should be engaged in these types of collaborative learning efforts. However, management should consider a number of potential obstacles to effectuate these processes in addition to the potential adverse effects that form their own cognitive biases.

Different in-group biases can arise where local managers and employees identify psychologically with a particular part of the multinational organization and thereby (unconsciously) favor initiatives, proposals, and projects that originate from those particular subgroups (Reitzig and Sorenson, 2013). This means that managers are scattered throughout the multinational corporation to serve as important liaisons between the operational frontline of the diverse organization and top management at headquarters. However, they may in fact communicate biased information that is skewed in favor of the perspectives that predominate within their own sub-unit. There is evidence that information brought forward and passed on to top management often is influenced by a particular management approach applied across or in specific parts within the organization. As a consequence, a hierarchical decentralized decision structure tends to reduce the flow of information passed on to top management because managers and employees "believe that their inputs are not taken seriously or are perceived as inappropriate" (Reitzig and Maciejovsky, 2014). In other words, the success of decentralization in multinational enterprises depends on the willingness of centralized decision makers to give up some of their power and display true openness and receptiveness to ideas generated from lower levels within the multinational corporation.

The leadership response to these insights obviously is to impose a more decentralized decision structure that increases the ability to engage in autonomous actions while enabling networked platforms for IT-enhanced communication and information exchanges and heeding the principles of openness and transparency across the organization.

Communication and control of the multinational corporation

The concept of *interactive control systems* is defined by four characteristics: (1) They are used regularly by top management, (2) they receive frequent attention by operating managers throughout the organization, (3) they entail face-to-face discussions between superiors and subordinates, and (4) they provide a platform for ongoing debate (Simons, 1991, 1994). Hence, the principles of interactive controls in many ways embrace the idea of interacting fast and slow processes of local responsiveness and forward-looking planning considerations while accommodating certain aspects of more open and transparent information-processing mechanisms. An interactive control system "enables top-level managers to focus on strategic uncertainties, to learn about threats and opportunities as competitive conditions change, and to respond proactively" (Simons, 1994: 81). That is, interactive controls can facilitate open dialogue between top managers at the corporate headquarters and subordinates located in local subsidiaries and business entities in direct personal discussions about the effects of responsive actions as a way to better comprehend developments in an uncertain environmental context. It can also be construed as a vehicle that is supportive of collective learning efforts by involving individuals with diverse experiences in open discussions that eventually can feed into the slow forward-looking strategic planning considerations.

The dynamic system constituted by the interaction between the slow long-cycled forward-looking reasoning at corporate headquarters and the fast short-cycled responses at the local overseas subsidiaries can be illustrated as a time-bound process enabled by management controls and IT-enhanced communication and information systems (Figure 7.1).

The long-term planning considerations at the multinational corporate headquarters constitutes a strategic-thinking process, looking at potential consequences multiple years ahead as a way to develop a general strategic direction for the corporation with specified mandates to each of the overseas subsidiaries in the multinational corporation. The shorter-term responsive consideration in the local business units engages in ad hoc responsive actions taken in view of observed changes in the local competitive environment to gain more immediate feedback as to what works and thereby experiment with alternative possibilities to test the way forward under uncertain

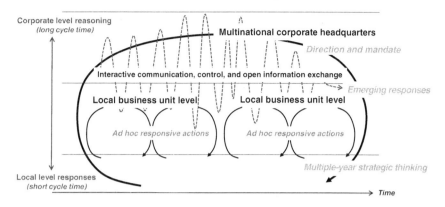

FIGURE 7.1 Interactive communication and control in the multinational corporation.

conditions. As time goes by and experiential insights are gathered from numerous responses throughout the multinational organization they are considered in the central planning process as possible solutions at the corporate level. This process is facilitated by more or less formalized interactive communication and control processes as well as informal information and knowledge exchange processes providing open access to all engaged parties located in different parts of the multinational corporation.

There must be effective interfaces at the intermediate tactical level to facilitate open discussions and information exchanges between the local operational managers and the strategic thinkers at corporate headquarters. It may entail regular budget discussions between local and corporate managers to better understand the environmental context when conditions evolve in uncertain ways in the form of an interactive control process (Simons, 1994). It may also comprise different information aggregation and crowdsourcing techniques to gather updated insights from actors in the frontline of the organizational periphery and forward this to top management at corporate headquarters (Hallin, 2016; Hallin et al., 2012; Hallin and Lind, 2016). In either case there is a need for frequent, if not ongoing, collaborative learning efforts as facilitating interfaces between the local operational responders and the central forward-looking thinkers based on the open exchange of information and knowledge. Hence, we need relatively high-frequency processes of interactive controls, open communication, and ongoing collaborative learning efforts to effectively bind the dynamic fast–slow processing system together.

The somewhat idealized depiction of the dynamic adaptive system implied by the interacting fast and slow processes, however, is not the norm among multinational corporations – even though the model is normative in nature, that is, it constitutes a recommended framework for effective conduct in turbulent global market contexts. The conditions around the dynamic interactive approach are often less than optimal. For example, many depictions of normal conduct in actual planning departments describe analytical reasoning constituted as simple updating and linear projections of past observations without open discussions of updated experiential knowledge from operations (e.g., Mintzberg 1994). We are also acutely aware of the many possible cognitive biases that can expose powerful executive decision makers and thereby exclude the consideration of valuable field observations. The internal communication may also furnish partially skewed information imposed by embedded biases that favor an informant's belonging to particular departments, functions, or geographical regions within the multinational corporation. As a consequence *weak signals* that indicate subtle emerging changes in the competitive environment are lost from the radar screen where closer attention to the updated experiences from local operations could provide important insights.

To move away from an unbalanced to a balanced centralized–decentralized system, decision makers in multinational corporations need to engage in *coordinating* decisions and processes *cultivating* employees globally to embark on autonomous initiatives. Some coordination efforts are central whereas others are decentralized. Coordination focuses on mutual adjustments to interrelated activities that need to be done, whereas cultivation is about dealing with the people who perform the activities they are good at and showing how they can help each other (Malone, 2004).

Coordination specifically involves three key conditions in multinational corporations: effective capabilities, aligned incentives and social connections that foster collaborative learning. Capabilities require that people have the skills needed to fulfill their jobs. In balanced centralized–decentralized structures many people are involved in evaluating candidates for jobs as it creates trust in the candidate across the global organization. Incentives are important in obtaining successful coordination. Incentives can be status, recognition, access to information or monetary compensation, including employee-ownership. Various incentives must be aligned and tailored to properly motivate the individual employee. Management should also consider the connections between activities and information, where peer-to-peer connections become important in more decentralized systems and top-down relations less important. Clearly communicated intent and goals also inspire and create motivation.

Cultivating is about harnessing the aims of employees in line with the organizational goals. This may sometimes require the corporation to adjust its strategies to match its goals, aims and abilities. This implies that the leadership sometimes must follow the people in the organization. For example, when the Internet programming language Java was designed by one of the best programmers at Sun Microsystems it was decided to give the programming language away for free as the demand for this language was low. However, free availability on the Internet made the program widely popular and Sun decided to reshape the whole strategy around this important asset. In other words, Sun cultivated the initiative and the abilities of the programmers to shape a new business strategy around Java. Another option to cultivate employees is to let people experiment and add more resources to those results that work well while other initiatives are turned down. Hence, the teams that are most successful in growing an innovation in the early stages are encouraged and the others are reassigned.

Managing business development based on the coordinating and cultivating principles can help the multinational corporation embark on a range of management approaches that are liberated from the conventional centralized mindset (Malone, 2004).

Effective collaborative learning promoted through cultivation hinges upon a supportive organizational culture with norms, values and behaviors that encourage and inspire ongoing discourse involving many individuals in all parts of the multinational organization. This comprises discussions around responsive actions in different operating entities and the associated experiential insights gathered from these endeavors at the local business entities, based on input from many involved employees with direct stakeholder contacts. So, engagement in local discourse should be encouraged and enabling communication and information systems connecting local business entities, specialized knowledge communities, and central planners at headquarters should be in place. The dynamic interactive fast–slow processing system implies open interfaces among all essential stakeholders including employees, managers, functional specialists, customers, suppliers, other external partners and collaborators. This organizational structure provides the means for direct updated feedback loops across many knowledgeable and engaged individuals, that will enhance general insight and understanding based on the collective intelligence that is accessible to the multinational corporation.

Collaborative learning requires an organizational setting where individual members can act and interact in a supportive social context that can only be fully understood by considering the role of organizational culture and its different artefacts. The implied norms and values will influence the way information is communicated and exchanged within the organization, including the treatment of updated insights from new experiences. Culture can be perceived as information that affects individual behaviors, which implies that there can be significant cultural variation around collective learning processes where individual information is exchanged openly in a social network (Boyd and Richerson, 2005). This also implies that multinational corporations, with the proper organizational culture to support effective collaborative learning processes, have accomplished a unique firm-specific feat that is valuable and inimitable as a source of sustainable competitive advantage.

The logic of the superior effects from dynamic interactive fast–slow processes in multinational corporations is based on individual motivation, collaborative learning and social network arguments. Here, learning and knowledge-creation is formed by individuals in groups that thrive on intent, autonomy and tension caused by fluctuation (Nonaka, 1994). Given the essence of this interactive dynamic, the essential leadership challenge is to enable it by forming an organization structure that can accommodate the dynamic and allow both fast and slow processes with appropriate communication and information systems to support it. Corporate leadership should simply enable effective fast–slow processing capabilities and establish an organizational culture conducive to open interaction and collaborative learning practices.

Both decentralized responsiveness and central analytical planning are important but must be balanced within a dynamic adaptive system. The global power generation and distribution company, AES Corporation, headquartered in Arlington, Virginia, is a prime example of an empowered organization with frontline autonomy to take responsive decisions. Yet, when demand conditions became more unfavorable in the early 2000s the company fell on hard times and was forced to impose more structure and central direction on its corporate business activities (Hamilton, 2003). The aggressive global expansion during the 1990s within a loose entrepreneurial structure lost economic focus under external pressures and was at the brink of Chapter 11 in 2002. Subsequently the corporate office was extended and overseas investments in power plants were trimmed, refocusing the corporate culture around responsibility, collaboration and individual excellence. Conversely, the strong central direction displayed at Sony Corporation, the Japanese electronics company that introduced the Walkman, lost its competitive edge momentarily and had trouble generating innovative business initiatives. A similar orientation on efficient production of competitive mobile phones to the world market seemed to demolish innovation in Nokia Corporation despite their undisputed engineering know-how and provided inroads for new competitors like Apple and Google. While these emerging business developments were observed by many individuals working inside the company, the weak signals from within were ignored or possibly dismissed by decision makers at corporate headquarters.

BOX 7.1 Interactive strategic human resource management in a multinational corporation

Chr. Hansen Holding (CHH) can be used as an example of a multinational corporation that has used its human resource management function to enable interactive strategy-making practices involving the corporate headquarters and engaging managers and employees in the overseas business entities (Andersen and Minbaeva, 2012). CHH was a rather successful operator in global food processing and pharmaceutical industries. It divested its food ingredients and color business to a private equity fund in 2005 and continued this business under the Chr. Hansen name (the company was listed on the NASDAQ OMX Nordic markets exchange in 2010). CHH was a nice and cozy workplace with a flat hierarchical structure and a friendly atmosphere. However, there was little accountability and focus on performance. To unleash the dormant potential in this knowledge-based organization the continuing company was transformed by adopting a clear strategic direction while at the same time engaging individual managers directly in the various local business initiatives throughout the multinational organization. This retained a decentralized structure but imposed a more central strategic focus in a structured process, incorporating local business initiatives as part of the formal management development process. That is, decentralization, local autonomy and empowerment was extended but at the same time complemented, with central direction and coordination processes creating a better balance between the center and local activities in the field.

The company established a new human resource department and developed management tools to support interactive strategy-making processes where top management could develop strategic understanding and direction to organizational members, while ensuring that experiences and insights derived from local initiatives were included in strategic considerations of top management (Figure 7.2).

The interactive processes provided the means to engage in regular discussions and exchanges between top management at headquarters and managers at the local business entities crossing hierarchical levels and geographical regions in accordance with sequential time dependent schedules. This provided opportunities to both discuss and deliberate openly about the competitive situation and strategic direction as well as considering the potential business opportunities to be derived from local responsive initiatives.

The human resource management processes imposed in practice served to facilitate both the central forward-looking planning deliberations at headquarters as well as the autonomous business initiatives taken at the overseas subsidiaries with a view to the local market opportunities. In addition to this the particular anchoring of these activities around the human resource department made the interactive practices a central part of the leadership development process where local managers and young talented employees were engaged much closer to the corporate strategy aims through direct

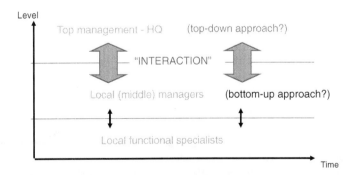

FIGURE 7.2 Interaction between top management and local managers in the multinational corporation.

encounters with top management. This became a highly effective and useful way to tailor future career paths to individual ambitions and corporate needs. It also provided regular opportunities to bring top management much closer to the business opportunities in the local markets and the initiatives taken to develop and exploit those for the corporation.

In essence the formal engagement in the central forward-looking planning discussions served to create a deeper commonly shared understanding of the global competitive situation and a strategic direction with long-term goals that provided guiding aspirations to the emerging business initiatives taken subsequently throughout the multinational organization (Figure 7.3).

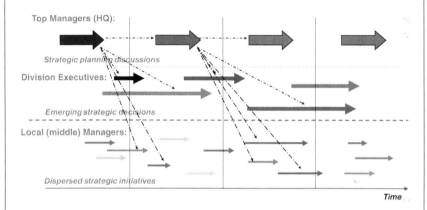

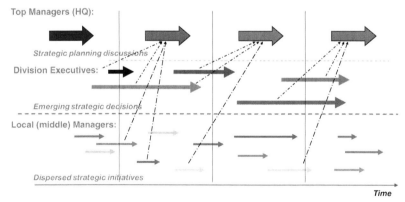

FIGURE 7.3 Interaction between corporate top-down and bottom-up communication processes.

The regular encounters to follow-up on various local strategic initiatives taken to exploit overseas market opportunities were used to provide inspiration to the central planning discussions. Hence, the human resource management process facilitated formalized and structured interactions between top management at the corporate headquarters, and managers and key employees in the local overseas subsidiaries, performed with regular time intervals as part of the internal career development policy.

The corporate human resource function implemented management practices that supported both central planning processes and decentralized strategic business initiatives. This comprised high-performance workshops organized in all the local overseas business entities with direct involvement of the CEO to foster open communication and create a common understanding about the corporate strategic direction. It also comprised local performance development interviews (PDIs) conducted around individual development plans with a view to concrete local business initiatives and their potential effects. This also incorporated periodic organizational audits (OAs) and organization reviews (ORs) conducted across all the local business entities as a way to discuss and bring local business initiatives to the direct attention of top management.

Multinational corporate leadership

The effective application of the interactive strategy-making approach, giving leeway for local autonomy in the multinational corporation, can be a challenge to the *leadership* role of the top management team that is considered to be the most influential group of decision makers at corporate headquarters. The corporate leadership must instill purpose, values and direction in the multinational corporation. It must promote rational forward-looking analytical reasoning, facilitating facts-based consideration using updated environmental insights to form a better understanding of the unfolding competitive reality. It must set up an organizational structure to enable autonomous responsive initiatives by decentralized managers operating in local business entities with different functional responsibilities and in different parts of the world. The people carrying out the central corporate planning activities and the dispersed individuals engaged in various responsive activities throughout the multinational organization should be combined through open IT-enhanced communication and information systems for ongoing informal exchanges of updated insights. This should coincide with open access and transparent formal management control systems that can support the interactive exchange of information and knowledge between central and decentralized local actors in the periphery of the multinational corporation. Hence, the role of the corporate leadership is very much linked to an ability to form an appropriate setting for the *responsive multinational corporation*

(RMC) with values, structures and systems that enhance the interaction be-tween fast and slow processes of immediate responses in local markets and consider forward-looking rationales to direct the corporate strategy.

Effective corporate leadership in the multinational organization should engage all actors in the corporation as potential contributors to the emerg-ing strategic outcomes. In this context, the strong and charismatic CEO as so often portrayed in the popular press, is somewhat misplaced. Charisma is typically conceived as an ability to persuade, excite, create high expecta-tions and pursue a strong personal vision. Good corporate performance is typically ascribed to good management, which, in turn, can be perceived as a form of leadership charisma but there is no evidence to suggest that strong leadership charisma by itself should lead to higher performance outcomes. Hence, the empirical evidence suggests that charismatic leaders generally are better compensated but make little difference to the corporate perfor-mance (Agle et al., 2006). Extravert leaders that manage in domineering, assertive, and loudly outspoken manners function better in front of passive employees but this style of management is associated with low performance outcomes when used to manage proactive, engaged employees (Grant et al., 2011). This is vividly illustrated in the case of Lehman Brothers and the total collapse of this large multinational corporation in September 2008, despite the dominant leadership of a visionary executive (Andersen, 2010).

Various studies suggest the best leaders do not have particular vision-ary abilities with unique predictive capabilities to outline the emerging future but, rather, constitute more disciplined, empirically oriented and concerned individuals (e.g., Collins and Hansen, 2011). This means that corporate leaders should abstract from convenient self-depiction as the main source of corporate strategic planning and focus more on a corporate setting that attracts all actors across the organization and engages them in experiments to find the right strategic responses. This opens up opportu-nities for more updated intelligence from the frontline of the organization that, if recognized by top management, can provide a basis for making the organization more democratic in the sense that it responds to insights from the periphery. There should be stronger ties between the strategic planning considerations and the actual business activities executed by many diverse individuals all the time and every day throughout the many parts of the multinational organization (e.g., Mintzberg, 2009). This obviously sets the stage for an interactive strategy-making approach combining fast responses in the field with slow forward-looking reasoning at the corporate center. Here the corporate leadership should engage the many organizational actors to be cognizant about subtle changes in market demands and con-sciously look for better responses that can address the changing competi-tive reality. Hence, successful organizations seem more consistent in their pursuit of internal actions where less successful companies are more in-clined to pursue aggressive growth initiatives imposed by top management at corporate headquarters (Collins and Hansen, 2011). The entrepreneurial search behavior among individuals operating in different parts of the multinational organization (see Chapter 2), and supported by corporate values and the distribution of decision-making power in the search to uncover emerging business opportunities, represent a viable solution to deal with the changing competitive context.

In increasingly dynamic and complex global business contexts it makes sense to engage the many individuals throughout the multinational organization in small stakes experiments that probe for the proper responses to emerging developments observed in the local task environments. As the relatively short-cycled experiences, obtained from these decentralized autonomous initiatives, come forward the related insights should be collected and agglomerated as updated information for the forward-looking strategic planning consideration at corporate headquarters. Hence, it is an important leadership challenge to form and enable the dynamic interaction between the ongoing autonomous actions taken by dispersed managers and employees throughout the multinational organization and the forward-looking planning considerations performed at the corporate center (Figure 7.4).

The central leaders typically operate out of the corporate headquarters, surrounded by various hierarchical managerial layers comprised by divisional executives, including various division heads that subsequently liaise with different operational managers in different parts of the multinational organization. Eventually, it is only the local managers that reach out to the frontline employees, who carry out all the corporate business transactions and thereby have a direct sense for what is happening and gradually

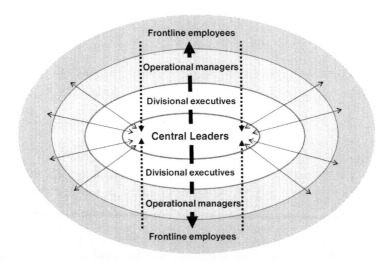

FIGURE 7.4   Interaction between the corporate center and peripheral managers and employees.

changing. This means that top management obtains an inordinate amount of information about the operational conduct of the multinational organization through the divisional executives that are next in line in the corporate hierarchy. The central leaders may have various contacts throughout the organization but the information channeled to the headquarters will inevitably be filtered by the interpretations of many managerial layers. This creates distance to the actual doings in the frontline around the organizational periphery and makes it difficult to be directly involved with all the ongoing doings of individual employees that are in immediate contact with many important stakeholders (Mintzberg et al., 2003). One way to deal with this challenge is to decentralize the decision structure and establish open communication channels for effective exchange of information, combined with transparent interactive control systems to integrate updated insights from peripheral responsive actions into the forward-looking planning considerations at the corporate center. Hence, Mintzberg (2009) argues that "the real planning of organizations takes place significantly in the heads of its managers and implicitly in the context of their daily actions." So, the interactive strategy-making process that combines insights from fast actions in the field with slow planning considerations at the center, tries to take advantage of the important engagement of dispersed managers that are close to the real business activities.

The current insights obtained from responsive initiatives in local business entities throughout the multinational corporation can contribute with updated knowledge that enlightens the analytical efforts in the central planning process to better comprehend the emerging changes in the global competitive environment. So, the multinational corporate entrepreneurial efforts can be based on the principles of *acting* and *creating* close to the actual business activities, as opposed to solely engaging in *thinking* and *analyzing* at the corporate center (Schlesinger and Kiefer, 2012). The combined perspective of fast updated field responses and slow central thinking in the interactive strategy-making process does not represent either–or choices but comprise complementary processes that must interact to create a dynamic adaptive system for the multinational corporation. Here the corporate leadership challenge is to orchestrate an open central planning process that enables decentralized responses throughout the multinational corporation and provides the means to gather updated information from the field with a willingness to use it. This way, the learning from doing develops new experiential insights from responsive experiments carried out in the local market contexts and can become an important source of updated environmental reconnaissance and intelligence in the rational forward-looking strategy analyses at the corporate center. Hence, it is an important leadership aspect to organize the interactive strategy-making processes with supportive communication and information systems to effectively integrate the fast decentralized and slow central process elements of the dynamic system.

The corporate leadership role should focus on the central formulation of a forward-looking strategic direction with a purpose, while enabling ensuing decision-making processes with sufficient autonomy to take responsive initiatives in view of emerging changes as a way to obtain updated market intelligence and a basis for adapting the corporate strategy to new environmental circumstances. This effectively allows strategic outcomes to be formed by responsive actions taken in different parts of the multinational corporation, in line with observed changes in the local market contexts. The corporate leadership should support a central planning process at headquarters to drive strategic intent while enabling and engaging individual organizational actors to pursue meaningful and responsive execution of the overarching strategic aims.

The corporate leadership role is not accomplished once the official strategy is formulated and sanctioned by the board while leaving the execution solely to the organization. Strategies are often seen as failing because they represent static documented statements and rationales disengaged from the actual business activities pursued by many organizational actors. Hence, corporate strategy-making entails close attention to ongoing execution with frequent interactive follow-ups considering the updated experiences derived from responsive initiatives taken in the field, as conditions and circumstances evolve often in different ways than anticipated in the prior planning. Executive decision makers are often heavily influenced by previous experiences that will color their sense-making capabilities, using analogies from the past to interpret strategic decision situations and impose expectations that everybody follows the executive lead (Gavetti and Rivkin, 2005; Pfeffer and Sutton, 2006). Even experienced top managers can be, and are often, distorted by various biases that can shape bad decisions where otherwise intelligent responsible people sometimes can make hopelessly flawed decisions despite the best information available (Campbell et al., 2009).

The prevailing beliefs of the corporate leadership must be challenged by the deep and updated insights residing with operating managers and employees working in direct contact with important stakeholders in the periphery of the multinational corporation. A leadership style that shows openness and an active search for alternative managerial opinions, promoting ideas and initiatives throughout the organization, have a positive effect on corporate performance (Torp, 2011). That is, effective strategy execution cannot be based solely on slavish implementation dictated by a preplanned path at headquarters. It must entail decentralized decision-making power with sufficient autonomy to engage in local responsive initiatives to deal with unexpected emerging circumstances in local markets, with transparency around an ongoing interactive process to constantly update the understanding of the turbulent global environment.

There must be room for the process of forming a corporate strategic direction from central, forward-looking analytical considerations at headquarters, as well as for the ability to take autonomous responsive initiatives in the local business operations. The two approaches must coexist and constitute balanced elements of the strategy-making process with equal emphasis. It is also important that the updated insights gained from the responsive initiatives throughout the multinational corporation are collected, communicated, and brought forward for ongoing considerations in the central planning process. This calls for a dynamic approach to managing financial resources so they can be allocated in the more flexible processes that leave room for improvisation and are not constrained by rigid application and approval procedures. This should restrain top management from imposing its own ideas on major resource-committing decisions without proper consultation from the deep expertise available among many diverse individuals inside the multinational corporation and thus avoid the worst effects of executive biases. In this context, lacking enthusiasm among local managers and employees does not necessarily signal disobedience and disengagement but is most likely an expression of genuine concern for the actions proposed by top management at the corporate center (Goold and Campbell, 1998).

More than three decades of research, focused on the performance effect of multinational corporate business activities, attests to the fact that some business diversity in related activities is associated with superior performance where sustainable value creation draws on common technological, business operation and information-processing capabilities. Some geographical diversification also has positive performance effects, particularly in knowledge-based industries that are less capital intensive where the advantages derive from an extended creativity and innovation potential that exceeds what is available to a purely domestic organization (Andersen, 2012). However, the ability to exploit those potential advantages requires that the diverse functional and geographical insights focused on the core business activities can be openly communicated and exchanged among organizational members at all levels, in all functions, and in all geographical locations across the multinational structure.

Hence, the leadership challenges require that appropriate structure, processes and systems in support of effective interactive strategy-making are established to allow the involvement of all organizational actors at all levels and all parts of the multinational corporation. However, in addition to this there is a need to impose core values and support the proper belief systems to guide the autonomous human interventions throughout the multinational corporation in line with overarching intent and purpose. The organizational culture reflects the accepted behaviors among individual actors and is influenced by the executive example (Schein, 2004), where concrete leadership actions must be pursued in accordance with prescribed principles. The priorities and principles practiced by corporate executives reflect their leadership style and shape the organizational climate that frames prevailing behaviors as managers and employees pursue a common cause. This means that top management, among other things, must instill an organizational culture of active participation, individual experimentation, creative behavior, innovation, and collaborative learning to improve and find new superior solutions to the emerging challenges of a turbulent global business environment.

Summary

Multinational corporate leaders are challenged to balance central coordination and decentralized decision-making supported by open communication and interactive controls. Coordinating and cultivating the business activities for local experimentation and collaborative learning through open worldwide information exchanges is just part of the answer. Effective leadership in the multinational corporation engages all organizational actors as potential contributors to the generation of innovative responses to emerging strategic issues. An effective centralized–decentralized interactive multinational corporation requires willingness among central decision makers to give up some of their power and show openness to engaged employees across the global organization.

References

Agarwal, R. and Helfat, C. E. (2009). Strategic renewal of organizations. *Organization Science*, **20**(2): 281–293.

Agle, B. R., Nagarajan, N. J., Sonnenfeld, J. A. and Srinivasan, D. (2006). Does CEO charisma matter? An empirical analysis of the relationships among organizational performance, environmental uncertainty, and top management team perceptions of CEO charisma. *Academy of Management Journal*, **49**(1): 161–174.

Andersen, T. J. (2010). Case: Lehman Brothers (B), Copenhagen Business School (available through the European Case Clearing House (ECCH)).

Andersen, T. J. (2012). Multinational risk and performance outcomes: Effects of knowledge intensity and industry context. *International Business Review*, **21**: 239–252.

Andersen, T. J. and Hallin, C. A. (2016). The adaptive organization. In Ramon J. Aldag (ed.) *Oxford Research Encyclopedias: Business and Management: A Community of Experts*. New York, NY: Oxford University Press.

Andersen, T. J. and Minbaeva, D. (2012). The role of human resource management in strategy making. *Human Resource Management*, **52**(5): 809–827.

Andersen, T. J., Denrell, J. and Bettis, R. A. (2007). Strategic responsiveness and Bowman's risk–return paradox. *Strategic Management Journal*, **28**(4): 407–429.

Bazerman, M. H. and Moore, D. A. (2008). *Judgment in Managerial Decision Making*. Hoboken, NJ: Wiley.

Boyd, R. and Richerson, P. J. (2005). *The Origin and Evolution of Cultures*. New York, NY: Oxford University Press.

Burgelman, R. A. (1991). Intraorganizational ecology of strategy making and organizational adaptation: Theory and field research. *Organization Science*, **2**(3): 239–262.

Campbell, A., Whitehead, J. and Finkelstein, S. (2009). Why good leaders make bad decisions. *Harvard Business Review,* **87**(2): 60–66.

Chakravarthy, B. S. (1982). Adaptation: A promising metaphor for strategic management. *Academy of Management Review,* **7**(1): 35–44.

Collins, J. and Hansen, M. T. (2011). *Great By Choice: Uncertainty, Chaos, and Luck – Why Some Thrive Despite Them All.* London, UK: Random House Business Books.

Crossan, M. M. and Berdrow, I. (2003). Organizational learning and strategic renewal. *Strategic Management Journal,* **24**(11): 1087–1105.

Galbraith, J. R. (1994). *Competing with Flexible Lateral Organizations.* Reading, MA: Addison-Wesley.

Galbraith, J. R. (1995). *Designing Organizations: An Executive Briefing on Strategy, Structure, and Process.* San Francisco, CA: Jossey-Bass.

Gavetti, G. and Rivkin, J. W. (2005). How strategists really think: Tapping the power of analogy. *Harvard Business Review,* **83**(4): 54–63.

Goold, M. and Campbell, A. (1998). Desperately seeking synergy. *Harvard Business Review,* **76**(5): 131–143.

Grant, A. M., Gino, F. and Hofmann, D. A. (2011). Reversing the extraverted leadership advantage: The role of employee proactivity. *Academy of Management Journal,* **54**(3): 528–550.

Hallin, C. A. and Lind, A. S. (2016). Strategic issue identification for crowd predictions. Paper presented at *The 2016 Collective Intelligence Conference, New York.*

Hallin, C. A. (2016). Aggregating predictions of operational uncertainties from the frontline: A new proactive risk management practice, in T. J. Andersen (ed.) *The Routledge Companion to Strategic Risk Management.* London: Routledge

Hallin, C. A., Andersen, T. J. and Tveterås, S. (2012). A prediction contest: The sensing of frontline employees against executive expectations. *Available at SSRN 2125878.*

Hamilton, M. M. (2003). AES's new power center: Struggling utility overhauls corporate (lack of) structure. *Washington Post,* Monday, June 2.

Kirschner, F., Paas, F. and Kirschner, P. A. (2009). A cognitive load approach to collaborative learning: United brains for complex tasks. *Educational Psychology Review,* **21**(1): 31–42.

Malone, T. (2004). *The Future of Work. How the Order of Business will Shape our Organization, Your Management Style and Your Life.* Boston, MA: Harvard Business School Press.

McGrath, R. G. (2013). *The End of Competitive Advantage: How to Keep Your Strategy Moving as Fast as Your Business.* Boston, MA: Harvard Business Review Press.

Mintzberg, H. (1994). The fall and rise of strategic planning. *Harvard Business Review,* **72**(1): 107–114.

Mintzberg, H. (2009). *Managing.* Harlow, UK: FT Prentice Hall.

Mintzberg, H., Lampel, J., Quinn, J. B. and Ghoshal, S. (2003). *The Strategy Process: Concepts, Contexts, Cases* (4th edition). Upper Saddle River, NJ: Pearson Prentice Hall.

Nonaka, I. (1994). A dynamic theory of organizational knowledge creation. *Organization Science,* **5**(1): 14–37.

Pfeffer, J. and Sutton, R. I. (2006). *Hard Facts, Dangerous Half-Truths & Total Nonsense.* Boston, MA: Harvard Business School Press.

Reitzig, M. and Maciejovsky, B. (2015). Corporate hierarchy and vertical information flow inside the firm – a behavioral view. *Strategic Management Journal*, **36**(13): 1979–1999.

Reitzig, M. and Sorenson, O. (2013). Biases in the selection stage of bottom-up strategy formulation. *Strategic Management Journal*, **34**(7): 782–799.

Schein, E. H. (2004). *Organizational Culture and Leadership* (3rd ed.). San Francisco, CA: Jossey-Bass.

Schlesinger, J. A. and Kiefer, C. F. (2012). *Just Start: Take Action, Embrace Uncertainty, Create the Future*. Boston, MA: Harvard Business Review Press.

Simons, R. (1991). Strategic orientation and top management attention to control systems. *Strategic Management Journal*, **12**(1): 49–62.

Simons, R. (1994). How new top managers use control systems as levers of strategic renewal. *Strategic Management Journal*, **15**(3): 169–189.

Torp, S. S. (2011). Employee stock ownership: Effect on strategic management and performance. PhD Dissertation, Copenhagen Business School.

8

DEMOCRATIZING THE MULTINATIONAL CORPORATION

Key points

- Advancing global strategic responsiveness
- Decentralized structure and adaptive processes
- The multinational corporate culture
- Honing the collective intelligence

This chapter recapitulates essential elements of the effective organizing of global business activities to achieve strategic responsiveness across a complex multinational corporation. In doing so, we emphasize the importance of the frontline agents who execute the business activities and introduce the notion of "democratizing" the strategic engagement of multinational managers and employees as a key feature of a new leadership paradigm in the responsive multinational corporation (RMC). In the implied *global strategic democracy*, all the critical decisions made in the RMC listen to the diverse insights and views of employees and other frontline stakeholders to achieve better-informed outcomes by tapping into the crowd wisdom readily available within the organization. Hence, the RMC acknowledges the collective intelligence contributed by everyone in the organization all of which have important insights that can be collected using information technology and exploited in conscious leadership efforts.

The ability to adapt the business activities in the multinational corporation to turbulent global business conditions is essential for retaining a competitive advantage where autonomy and strategic response capabilities are some of the normative prescriptions (e.g., Bettis and Hitt, 1995; McGrath, 2013). These general recommendations are appealing but it is not at all clear how they should be applied in practice in complex multinational contexts where effective strategic adaptation is somehow linked to the interaction between central coordination at headquarters and decentralized responses in local business entities. If organizations fail to adapt it is often ascribed to poor implementation of the strategic plans where, in reality, it is top management that have failed to both engage actively in the ongoing execution of the strategy projects and consider how dynamic changes and unexpected development affect the need for updated actions (e.g., Hrebiniak, 2005; Speculand, 2009).

From an evolutionary perspective the autonomous business initiatives taken within the organization are seen as necessary precursors to subsequent strategic adaptation where *intent* is the directive prelude provided by top management without any need for involvement in the actual execution of business activities (e.g., Lovas and Ghoshal, 2000; Mirabeau and Maguire, 2014). So, while it is generally recognized that strategy-making entails both strategic intent and emergence (Mintzberg and Waters, 1985) it is not always clear how these central and decentralized processes are integrated. To this end, we propose that the adaptive multinational corporation (RMC) should pursue an interactive strategy-making model that combines forward-looking reasoning of central planning with updated insights from decentralized responses taken in the different operating entities of the organization (Andersen, 2015; Andersen and Hallin, 2016). It is the interaction between these central and decentralized processes that constitute the adaptive system whereby strategy becomes a democratized process where corporate actions take into account the collective intelligence of all actors within the multinational corporation.

Democracy is generally considered a highly legitimate form of government, generally heeded by our Western societies as being fair and rather effective, at least relatively speaking (Landemore, 2013). The word democracy derives from the two Greek words "demos" and "kratein," which is translated into "rule by the people" (Encyclopedia Britannica, 2016). However, the governance of democracy is typically limited to electing senior officials for public office around deliberating parliamentary settings. For example people may elect a president, but the president is then the leader of a formal hierarchical bureaucracy with established governmental institutions. The population also elect parliamentary representatives who in turn will discuss and vote on various laws where the implementation of laws is executed by hierarchically organized public agencies. Many multinational corporations operate within a comparable governing structure. The stockholders elect a board of directors, the board members vote on policies, and the business policies are executed within a hierarchically organized structure. A main difference obviously is that the voting rights to elect the corporate boards are reserved for the owners of company stock and typically allocated on a pro rata basis with more votes allocated to those who own more shares. The global strategic democracy is a different type of governance mechanism that can be imposed to ensure that important strategic decisions taken at the corporate center by top management and sanctioned by the board of directors will consult the collective intelligence of the people operating inside the organization. This is not just a new approach to get better-informed strategic decisions in the RMC but it also has the potential to motivate and amplify the human potential scattered across the organization as a whole.

We use the term global strategic democracy to pinpoint the potential advantages demonstrably associated with participatory decision-making and the inclusion of collective decision procedures to inform important resource committing decisions (e.g., Eisenhardt, 1989; Hong and Page, 2001, 2004). That is, procedures for collecting aggregated views and assessment directly from all members of the multinational corporation to inform and guide important central decisions can be very useful. The potential benefits of global strategic democracy partially derive from the ability to impose more *reliable* decision-making procedures because it promotes *deliberation*. According to Manin (2005: 14) deliberation has two implications for decisions. One is that deliberation where decision issues are weighed in the minds of many will foster more careful attention to the underlying issues and concerns. Another is that the quality of these considerations, regarding reasons for and against, is a function of the number of councilors involved in the deliberations. In other words, the wisdom of the internal crowd can be an excellent informant.

There are arguably three main properties that lead to the ascribed advantages of global strategic democracy, that hold a promise of making the multinational corporation more responsive in the face of changes in the global business context (cf. Landemore, 2013). First, soliciting the internal crowd of agents will enlarge the pool of information, insights and ideas from which to gather relevant intelligence. By aggregating the sensed impressions of frontline stakeholders, new current and fully updated insights can be made available that otherwise would be overlooked in strategic decisions. Second, the more insights and ideas available, the higher the likelihood that invalid arguments are uncovered and discarded while good and valid arguments are being advanced. Hong and Page (2001, 2004) contrast the logic of using collective intelligence in problem-solving to the nature of decisions between few people and find that the cognitive diversity of the many insights trumps the ability of individuals, no matter how skilled. Third, the consensus based on the "voting" of the frontline stakeholders can ensure "better" and more "reasonable" solutions. In other words, involving a large number of insightful people in problem-solving will provide greater cognitive diversity (Landemore, 2012) that increases the likelihood of finding good solutions and/or of choosing the best solutions among alternative options.

Hence, four important considerations surface with respect to the pursuit of global strategic democracy. First, how can the RMC instill a proper organizational context through specific structural and processual features? Second, how should the RMC determine which problem-solving tasks to centralize at headquarters and which to decentralize to the overseas subsidiaries? Third, how does the RMC ensure that the collective decisions are always "wise"? That is, how do we avoid the influences of trends and fads where groups sometimes make dumb decisions (Landemore, 2012). Fourth, what traits of the organizational culture are likely to advance collective intelligence and thereby promote higher responsiveness in the RMC? In the following, we discuss these four issues to identify proper organizational and leadership features to boost collective wisdom and avoid collective stupidity to the benefit of strategic responsiveness.

The need for global strategic democracy in the RMC

A decentralized decision-making structure enables immediate local responses but does not ensure sustainable corporate performance outcomes. The diverse organizational responses must be coordinated and integrated into cohesive strategic activities within an efficient multinational operating structure to achieve durable economic outcomes. The challenge then is to employ global strategic democracy in ways that enable a proper balance between combined central planning processes and decentralized responses taken by autonomous actors throughout the organization.

As decentralized initiatives gain momentum and show positive results, they can eventually become part of the official corporate strategy as local managers promote and champion the successful ventures to top management at corporate headquarters. This reflects an evolutionary perspective where responsive initiatives are taken by actors in the operational echelons of the organization where the primary top management role is to organize and structure the multinational corporation to furnish this process effectively. The prevalence of decentralized initiatives is also reflected in the concept of *guided evolution* (Lovas and Ghoshal, 2000) even though top management here fulfills a more visible role by formulating the strategic intent that guides the various initiatives taken within the organization. However, the development of strategic intent "is exogenous to the evolutionary and ecological process" and rather reflects top management's preconceived "vision" formed by "their conception of the external environment" (Lovas and Ghoshal, 2000: 886). The evolutionary perspective then sees the autonomous initiatives of operational managers as the source of strategic renewal where experimentation with different approaches is selected by the environmental reality and successful ventures promoted as future strategies. But, this depiction of the strategy-making process has little consideration for potential interactions between top management at headquarters and frontline managers and employees in global subsidiaries.

A decentralized decision structure allows autonomous initiatives to be taken at the operating units in the organization where the business activities are carried out in direct contact with various frontline stakeholders. The responses are taken in view of changing environmental conditions where, say, customer demands might be changing, a new technology is being applied, etc. In other words, the responses are enacted as a consequence of observations in the local task environments and the engaged actors learn about the business context through direct interactions with key stakeholders. This resembles the phenomenon of *knowledge creation* discussed by Nonaka, Toyama and Hirata (2008: 8–10) describing "a process created and used in relation with the knowledge of other human beings" where the knowledge "is created by people in their interactions." Hence, the ability to innovate and renew requires enactment in practice where the new insights represent tacit knowledge communicated as shared experiences. As a consequence, the new experiences must be communicated and shared across management layers to obtain sufficient backing from top management where the updated insights and initiatives represent sources of strategic renewal and sustainable differentiation.

Nonaka et al. (2008) see the primary leadership role as expressing the strategic intent to the organizational actors and creating a proper setting for knowledge creation ("ba"). Bungay (2011) refers to *directed opportunism* as a somewhat comparable concept inspired by the fast adaptive practices developed in the Prussian Army in the 19th century. Given that battlefields always lead to unforeseeable circumstances, people at all levels of command must be able to act on their own initiative when needed in line with the overarching intent. Strategy is here seen as "a framework for decision making" conceived as "direction, which enables subsequent choices about action" (Bungay, 2011: 97–98). In short, it implies that "strategy develops further as action takes place" (Bungay, 2001: 102). This tells us that strategy evolves as ongoing knowledge-creation, or learning-by-doing, where emergent actions respond to the evolving unforeseen developments as new initiatives with potential long-term strategic impact. Similarly, the emergent strategy-making process described by Mirabeau and Maguire (2014) builds on a view of strategy as an evolutionary process of iterated resource allocations.

These strategy perspectives all point to the importance of improvised responses in view of uncertain and unpredictable conditions and they recognize the important leadership role of creating the right overarching strategic intent to guide those actions. However, none of these perspectives that largely derive from detailed longitudinal case studies consider the importance of interaction between top management at the corporate center and responding managers in peripheral operating units. One of the reasons might be that the case studies have been confined to analyzing the evolution of business ventures and emerging strategic initiatives where interactive processes are absent. Hence, Bromiley and Rau (2014: 1253) point out that "strictly qualitative research has a limited ability to identify effective processes rigorously." In other words, since studies of venturing and emergence focus on the dynamic life of autonomous business initiatives they do not consider the role of top management as being actively involved in forward-looking planning where their strategic deliberations can be updated by the current environmental insights from local field experiences. Nonetheless, Burgelman and Grove (1996) discuss that top management needs to actively liaise between the analysis of the changing competitive reality and emerging autonomous initiatives that may prove to be the right strategic responses for the corporation.

A critique of the evolutionary approach recognizes some shortcomings, such as the fact that top management might develop a flawed vision that can lead to a misleading strategic intent (Lovas and Ghoshal, 2000). This can lead to mal-adaptation of business activities and poorly focused response initiatives on sustainable benefits. In this context, evolutionary theory assumes that self-organizing systems can make sense of the chaotic environment as every employee performs experiments as a survival strategy. However, it can be difficult for decision makers to understand the reasons for success and may lead to disorganization, imposing extensive costs on the organization (Recanatini and Ryterman, 2000). Moreover, when self-organized complex systems create stress from constant evolution, the system becomes unstable, and employees experience reduced work motivation (Bloom and Michael, 2002). In short, to sustain competitive advantage the RMC must apply a form of global strategic democracy within a system that relies both on central coordination and dispersed insights and ideas within a balanced centralization–decentralization structure (cf. Malone, 2004).

Enabling global strategic democracy through structures and processes

New information technologies enable aggregation of crowd predictions and collective intelligence using online opinion polling and voting among frontline stakeholders. In Chapter 4 we discussed sensing of the business environment by frontline stakeholders that allows for the aggregation of collective judgments as a basis for environmental reconnaissance and intelligence-gathering. The frontline stakeholders perceive weak signals relatively quickly from their daily work where they interact directly with key stakeholders and observe their reactions. The frontline stakeholders sense weak signals from people within their individual networks, both through online connections and direct personal relations. The ability to gather information from a broader set of constituents can gain more precise predictions, capturing the "wisdom of the crowds" (Surowiecki, 2004). This updated sensing information can be gathered from prediction markets where stakeholders virtually invest in different strategic decisions (e.g., Wolfers and Zitzewitz, 2004) or from online surveys without markets (Hallin, 2016; Hallin et al., 2012, 2013a, 2013b; Hallin and Lind, 2016). These kinds of prediction platforms can be used to aggregate sensing information, make predictions, identify consensus and conduct votes with respect to specific decisions and expected outcomes.

In a corporate setting, relevant decision-making problems for "voting" in a global strategic democracy could be choosing a new CEO, local subsidiary managers, line managers, or other important strategic decisions including new corporate policies, mergers, acquisitions, new market entry, etc. These types of decisions are notoriously set within the responsibility of top management and the board and constitute *high-stakes* decisions where the outcomes can have a major positive or negative effect on future performance. In these situations it is only prudent to gain the view of the collective intelligence inside the organization to guide the decisions. Opinion polling is another aggregation model that can be applied to gather the views and opinions of the frontline stakeholders. Opinion polling is already a well-known procedure but tends to focus on more mundane applications, such as, obtaining regular feedback on predetermined employee satisfaction surveys and the like. In contrast, opinion polling with respect to strategic decisions is a new application to most companies. But there are exceptions. Hewlett-Packard (HP) engaged in a dynamic opinion poll to survey employees on the decision to acquire Compaq Computer in late 2001. They acknowledged that the 86,000 employees would be instrumental to a successful merger between HP and Compaq Computer, which often hinges upon compatible organizational cultures. So, they conducted periodic opinion polls to gauge feelings about the acquisition where the last survey showed a consensus among employees in support for the deal (Malone, 2002).

A decentralized decision structure cultivates global strategic democracy by moving power down the organization so operating managers in the frontline can take responsive initiatives within their areas of responsibility and learn about the environment directly from those experiences. This gives influence to people closer to the relevant information and expertise and gives them the opportunity to voice their opinions so it can be considered quickly under unforeseen circumstances (e.g., Child and McGrath, 2001; Daft and Lewin, 1993; Volberda, 1998). This provides the very basis for individual sensing of experiential insights among frontline stakeholders that can be used as input to make regular electronic predictions and arrange pooling surveys with respect to specific strategic decisions. In decentralized organizations decisions can be more readily made by local decision makers in view of the changing conditions and thereby instigate proper and fast responses. The fast responses generate experiential insights where the local managers relatively quickly find out what works and what does not work under new circumstances. They receive feedback directly from the stakeholders involved, such as, colleagues, employees, managers, customers, suppliers, partners, etc. These insights gained by local managers and employees, generate updated information about environmental changes and constitute important information to enlighten the conceptual knowledge of top management at the corporate center.

The frontline around the periphery of the multinational corporation is particularly complex because it entails different business and functional operations and these activities are scattered across diverse overseas markets that represent a fertile ground for democratizing the frontline stakeholders (Figure 8.1). This provides opportunities to gain first-hand sensing insights from frontline employees in each of the markets with further access to external frontline stakeholders among customers, suppliers and other partners as sources for updated global market intelligence.

The coordination between dispersed local business entities and multiple business initiatives across the world is an essential consideration in global strategic democracy. Coordination typically happens as part of the slow forward-looking reasoning in the strategic planning process that requires the sharing of updated experiential information from local operating managers exchanged through horizontal communication and management control systems. The ability to communicate effectively among organizational members with different types of expertise and insights is a precondition for collective learning and innovative capabilities that takes advantage of diverse knowledge, insights and expertise. This can be carried out in multiple ways ranging from regular conference meetings, interactive control sessions, and informal conversations between individuals across overseas business entities.

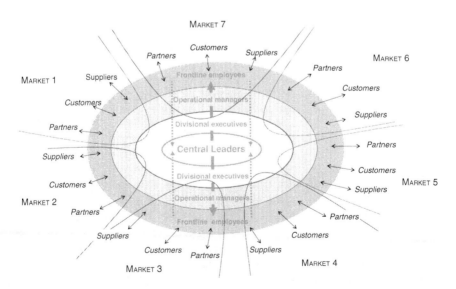

FIGURE 8.1 Democratizing the multinational corporation engaging frontline stakeholders.

Global strategic democracy is promoted through informal spontaneous collaborative learning processes among many individuals in the multinational organization. The collaborative learning approach enhances creativity and develops viable solutions to complex strategic issues where the cognitive limitations of individual thinkers can be circumvented by drawing on broad and diverse knowledge sources (Kirschner et al., 2009). Hence, the interactive information-sharing obtained through formal interactive control systems (e.g., Simons, 1994), or informal exchange of information and knowledge through lateral communication channels, can ensure that diverse updated insight is processed among many individuals from different parts of the RMC to facilitate collaborative learning. It also facilitates information exchanges between fast responsive actions and slow forward-looking reasoning in the fast–slow dynamic to obtain better and more adaptive strategic decisions.

In line with the fast–slow processing rationale, we suggest that corporate executives consider the current insights from experiential learning generated both from frontline managers at the operational level of the organization as well as from relevant frontline stakeholders of the multinational organization. This information can be obtained by employing different methodologies including prediction aggregation, electronic voting, and online polling surveys. The sensing of frontline stakeholders can also be collected systematically using different crowdsourcing and prediction techniques (e.g., Hallin, 2015; Hallin et al., 2012, 2013a, 2013b; Hallin and Lind, 2016). Information-sharing between corporate executives, local managers and frontline employees should include these kinds of regular sensing aggregation mechanisms although in principle they also may follow informal channels directly from engaged employees to top management or transmitted through middle-managers. However, we know that middle managers for various reasons filter the information that is brought forward to top management as well, as in most organizations it is difficult to reach the CEO directly by phone or email. Hence, the polling mechanisms are a good way to obtain frontline information and make it available to top management.

We, therefore, need relatively high-frequency interactive processes where collaborative learning can flourish, supported by democratizing interventions that can bind the fast–slow processing system together through frequent information updating, ongoing monitoring, open communication and interactive discussions. This is the crux of global strategic responsiveness. The organization must find a proper balance between periodic management reporting, interactive controls and informal communication and information exchange mechanisms. This combination must be tailored to serve the firm-specific needs and geared to specific industry conditions, which in turn can become a winning formula for sustainable competitive advantage in the form of unique strategic response capabilities.

Decentralized decision delegation

The interactive strategy-making process goes beyond the simple emergent learning view by consciously focusing on the time-bound interaction between central forward-looking strategy considerations at headquarters and the current experiences gained from decentralized responsive actions in the local business entities. Here strategic intent is not a one-directional vision that guides emergent activities. The intended plans give direction to ongoing responsive actions and the strategic intent in turn is being influenced by open discussions informed by updated insights derived from the decentralized responses. It is this ongoing interaction that forms the basis for a dynamic adaptive system.

The true leadership challenge is to enable this dynamic interactive system by encouraging both fast and slow processes, and establishing management information and control processes to facilitate the necessary interaction between them in a complex multinational setting. We know that corporate managers differ in their ability to deal with environmental changes where the implied *dynamic managerial capabilities* defined as "capabilities with which managers build, integrate, and reconfigure organizational resources and competences" (Adner and Helfat, 2003: 1020) will influence the strategic outcomes of the firms they manage. Hence, top management should be actively engaged in discussions about updated information gathered from low-level managers and the frontline employees involved directly in the daily execution of the firm's business activities, because they are the first to know what happens. As noted by Hrebiniak (2005: 9–11) "strategic success demands a 'simultaneous' view of planning and doing" and in reality execution is influenced by "integrated decisions and actions over time." It may be an executive shortcoming as argued by Speculand (2009: 8): "Leaders feel that after they have crafted their strategy, they can move on ... that is not the case." Hence, the central leaders at corporate headquarters should use strategic intelligence from the local managers and frontline employees as essential input to forward-looking strategic planning discussions. The central leaders should promote fast–slow processing capabilities and support an organizational culture that is conducive to open interaction, information sharing and collaborative learning practices. This means that top management must impose proper decision structures, communication and information systems enhanced by supportive corporate values, behavioral guidelines, and consistent incentive systems.

The RMC thrives on the interaction between slow reasoning at the center at corporate headquarters and fast insights obtained from the organizational periphery at the local subsidiaries that constitute the fast–slow multinational dynamic adaptive system (Figure 8.2). The corporate headquarters at the center primarily focus on the centralized concerns about the crucial infrastructure required to run a flexible, robust, and resilient multinational operating structure with supportive corporate processes of management controls, global communication and information systems. The center at corporate headquarters provides the *Mandate* to each of the overseas subsidiaries as a general guide to the execution of business activities in the local markets. The local subsidiaries operating in the organizational periphery focus on strategy execution in the local markets and take responsive initiatives in view of ongoing changes in the market and pursue business development that caters to those changing conditions. The local subsidiaries in the organizational periphery provide an *Update* to the corporate headquarters, with local market intelligence informed by the experiential insights obtained from the ongoing responsive initiatives and business development efforts that are geared to the local markets.

So, the RMC must have a balanced centralized–decentralized interactive adaptive system. At one end, there is a need for controlled, hierarchical multinational structures and processes. For example, Walmart and Amazon operate business models that require tight infrastructures and processes to gain economic scale and scope efficiencies (Ticoll, 2004). At the other end, there are self-organizing business entities with no central control over operations. For example, eBay is a trading platform where participants can interact in a marketplace deciding themselves what is being traded, the prices offered, and so on. Wikipedia is another example of a self-organized entity without a formal hierarchical structure where the users collectively determine the contents through their own initiatives but following general guidelines for content development. However, all multinational corporations fall somewhere between the centralized hierarchy and the decentralized self-organization and there has to be a suitable balance between centralized structure and the decentralized initiatives. Both are required to obtain an effective dynamic adaptive system.

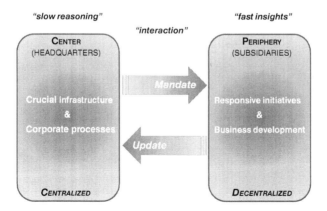

FIGURE 8.2 The adaptive interacting central and peripheral processes in the multinational corporation.

There are several factors to consider when deciding on the decentralization–centralization equation across different multinational corporate functions and tasks (Malone, 2004). In each case, the potential benefits of decentralization in terms of fast initiatives, flexible responses, updated insights, motivation, creativity, etc. must be weighed against the benefits of centralization, such as, economic efficiency, simplicity, quality, risk management, etc. These are trade-offs unique to each organization. In situations where decisions economize on communication costs and solve basic conflicts of interest, centralized decisions may be more efficient. In areas where decisions require high motivation, tapping into many minds with respect to innovation and new ventures, decentralized decisions may be more effective. That is, in most cases it is relevant to tailor differentiated decision structures to deal with different types of decisions. Hence, in the context of the multinational corporation, we can distinguish between functional areas that typically are the responsibility of corporate headquarters and other functions that are more effectively looked after by the local subsidiaries (Figure 8.3).

For example, the strategic planning process with the aim of establishing an overarching purpose and intent for corporate actions, while staking out coordinated strategic activities at the corporate level, typically fall under the auspices of the corporate headquarters. Similarly, it takes a higher level decision-node to consider the best multinational operating structure for the RMC, including associated restructuring, and M&A decisions, often surrounded by secrecy and confidentiality restrictions, are similarly confined to corporate headquarter responsibilities. Conversely, it makes sense to allocate decision-making power to local subsidiaries on almost anything

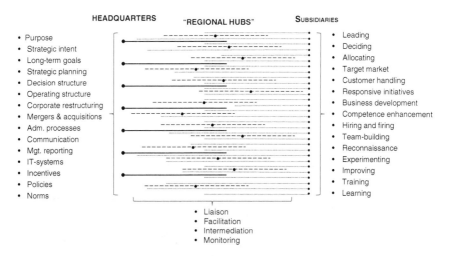

FIGURE 8.3 Possible distribution of functional responsibilities in the multinational corporation.

that relates to addressing the local market needs and conditions, including recruitment, training, customer handling, business development efforts, etc. An interesting thing to note of course is that, even though the decision-making responsibility may be delegated, there can still (and should) be open communication and information transparency around all decisions, which will enhance the interaction between central and decentralized business entities and functional units. We can also think of different divisional-level or matrix-type responsibilities (call those "regional hubs" for lack of a better word) that may function as managerial liaison mechanisms between center and periphery with some, or no, decision-making power delegated to accomplish intermediation activities.

The prior success of the Hewlett-Packard Company (HP) during the period of the initial founders may illustrate the balance between the centralized and the decentralized functional responsibilities. The success that catapulted HP into its past impressive success can be ascribed to a central structure with corporate values that nurtured decentralized initiative with an urge to let them persevere. The general principle was that the development of business opportunities was made as low as possible in the organization close to the market, customers and end-users. Only crucial infrastructure and corporate processes should be maintained under central coordination (Andersen, 2013; House and Price, 2009).

We also note, of course, that the operationalization of the centralization–decentralization balance is enhanced by the presence of effective global communication and information technologies and an organization culture that encourages the open use of these means for collaborative and creative purposes. Furthermore, the balance can be eased by utilizing the techniques of global strategic democracy, thus allowing updated intelligence from the wisdom of internal crowds to inform and even guide central strategic decisions to the benefit of the RMC.

Honing collective wisdom and avoiding collective stupidity

The fast experiential insights gained by frontline stakeholders can be collected for consideration in the strategic-thinking process around top management (Figure 8.4). The active execution of business transactions by employees in operating units forces frontline employees to respond to ongoing changes in their task environments where they learn from these adjustments through trial and error learning and thereby obtain new insights and knowledge about the changing business context. This information from frontline sensing among engaged employees is a potential source of competitive advantage if it is used to react faster to emerging trends compared to close competitors in the industry. The information constitutes potential environmental intelligence, identifying emergent risks, new business opportunities, and possibly creative responses to deal better with the changing conditions.

The collective intelligence from the frontline provides an opportunity to gain updated information about subtle environmental changes that otherwise might go unnoticed by the executives at corporate headquarters. Top managers are typically informed about internal organizational matters by the middle management layers but in reality they serve as a horizontal communication filter where only selective bits of information get through. The unique access to updated global market intelligence provides a convenient way to challenge preconceived perceptions derived from ingrained conversations among like-minded peers. This provides the means to challenge potential biases and misperceptions (e.g., Bazerman and Moore, 2008), dominant logics of key opinion leaders (Bettis and Prahalad, 1995) and address possible sources of organizational inertia (e.g., Hannan and Freeman, 1989). However, it is also a precondition that leadership shows receptiveness or a willingness to actually consider the frontline information, which is not always the case for various reasons.

Hence, the ability to utilize the collective intelligence of the frontline depends on a particular leadership style that hones corporate democratic values of openness, transparency, participation, collective learning, etc. It also hinges on the decentralization of decisions on local operations with an effective communication and information system to exchange insights and knowledge across individuals in different hierarchical, functional and geographical locations.

It is important that aggregated information from frontline stakeholders and responsive initiatives are shared between the local subsidiaries and the corporate center. Burgelman and Grove (1996) describe the challenge associated with the introduction of Intel's new microchip strategy in the early 1980s when the competitive situation changed and top management was unaware that an engineer had developed this new business opportunity

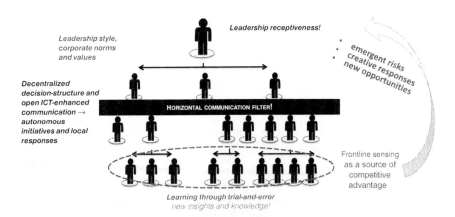

FIGURE 8.4   Using the collective intelligence of frontline employees to inform top management.

(Grove, 1996). Pascale (1984, 1996) similarly discusses how Honda's entry into the US market was based on the responsive actions of the local managers in California, who learned along the way what worked in the market, partly by accident, and where these experiences and insights were considered in the subsequent corporate strategy after the fact.

The collective wisdom is the core of any social and societal endeavor (Landemore and Elster, 2012). People as social beings gather together because they know they can achieve more as a group than being alone and make decisions collectively in the expectation that those decisions are better than the decisions made by one or a few individuals. So, the collective wisdom can outperform judgments by the few. However, there is also evidence that the opposite can happen. Charles Mackay (1841) referred to "the madness of crowds," claiming that "too many cooks spoil the broth." This attitude is not uncommon in political science from Plato to modern democrats where a dominant argument is that many are incapable of taking any kind of smart decisions. We also note occasional periods of herd behaviors in financial markets and real estate where "collective stupidity" can lead to price bubbles. Bubbles can be powered by destructive self-reinforcing feedback loops.

In multinational organizations, the same tendency can be present in the form of group thinking. That is, employees and frontline stakeholders can influence each other through frequent communication, manipulation and group pressure (e.g., Luckner, 2008). Hence, it is important to overcome potential collective biases to safeguard the collective intelligence. Hong and Page (2001, 2004) refer to four principles that must be fulfilled to obtain effective groups for collective intelligence. *Diversity* – members of the (smart) group must allow diversity of opinions. *Decentralization* – members draw on specialized or localized knowledge. *Independence* – the members are able to express themselves without being affected by the others. *Aggregation* – an independent mechanism exists to add the information together. The RMC can live up to these criteria by including frontline participants in different operating functions in many diverse locations including individuals engaged directly in the daily business activities. Employees in different locations develop localized knowledge that is independent of information obtained in other regions and derived from their unique experiences working with local stakeholders unaffected by opinions in other foreign subsidiaries. The online information technologies provide effective ways to aggregate predictions with software platforms that work as an independent mechanism. That is, there are ways to avoid the phenomenon of collective stupidity in the multinational corporation where much of the intelligence is anchored locally.

Organizational culture and responsiveness

Cultural evolution provides an adaptive mechanism for social systems including organizations and societies. The ability for collaborative learning is therefore not just a byproduct of individual learning but constitutes distinctly human "special-purpose mental mechanisms" (Boyd and Richerson, 2005: 100). The ability to engage in decentralized responses or autonomous initiatives and sharing the experiential insights obtained from these in open collaborative learning is a culturally driven process. It constitutes an economical way to handle uncertain and unpredictable business environments. This dynamic learning process identifies effective responses from small experiments and trial-and-error learning that can be shared for possible application in other parts of the organization.

The fast–slow systems thinking derived from modern science provides a better understanding of the organizational processes required to generate effective strategic adaptation in the multinational corporation. But, it also raises new questions about how top managers and corporate leaders can enable the embedded interactive strategy-making processes by a strong culture supporting collaborative learning and open interaction. The fast system of decentralized responses requires sufficient organizational slack to give leeway for spontaneous experiments. This can be at odds with alternative requirements for economic efficiencies. Collaborative learning also requires openness to consider the updated information and encourage open discussions among diverse stakeholders. However, the normative interactive strategy-making model can only be achieved if corporate leadership is willing to back it.

The ability to invoke dynamic capabilities in the multinational corporation requires individual cognitive capabilities among executives, managers and other organizational members operating throughout the multinational corporation (Teece, 2007, 2009). The adaptive strategy dynamic thrives on central and decentralized processes with multi-layered networks of divisional, line and local managers and frontline employees that can be a source for updated environmental intelligence brought to the attention of top management. It is this open interaction across hierarchical, functional and geographical divides in the multinational corporation that brings current local market insights to the attention of central strategy discussions at corporate headquarters when considering coordinated adaptive actions. This behavior, based on open exchange of experiential insights and updated market information, can be an engrained element of the organizational culture and constitutes an effective way to adapt. Hence, interactive strategy-making can enable effective strategic adaptation in the multinational corporation in the face of turbulent global business conditions.

Summary

The ability to form a dynamic responsive system across the multinational corporation builds on interactive strategy-making that combines fast autonomous local responses and slow forward-looking strategic reasoning at headquarters. We argue that global strategic democracy complements these structures and processes to facilitate updated market intelligence from individuals in the frontline to top managers at corporate headquarters. The RMC requires leadership focus on corporate values, purpose, a decentralized decision structure, communication and information technology. Adhering to the collective intelligence principles enables collaborative learning and crowdsourcing for updated intelligence that foster a global strategic democracy.

References

Adner, R. and Helfat, C. E. (2003). Corporate effects and dynamic managerial capabilities. *Strategic Management Journal*, **24**(10): 1011–1025.

Andersen, T. J. (2013). *Short Introduction to Strategic Management*. Cambridge, UK: Cambridge University Press.

Andersen, T. J. (2015). Interactive strategy-making: Combining central reasoning with ongoing learning from decentralized responses. *Journal of General Management*, **40**(4): 69–88.

Andersen, T. J. and Hallin, C. A. (2016). The adaptive organization. In Ramon J. Aldag (ed.) *Oxford Research Encyclopedias: Business and Management: A Community of Experts*. New York, NY: Oxford University Press, 2016.

Bazerman, M. H. and Moore, D. A. (2008). *Judgment in Managerial Decision Making*. New York, NY: Wiley.

Bettis, R. A. and Hitt, M. A. (1995). The new competitive landscape. *Strategic Management Journal*, **16**(S1): 7–19.

Bettis, R. A. and Prahalad, C. K. (1995). The dominant logic: Retrospective and extension, *Strategic Management Journal*, **16**(1): 5–14.

Bloom, M. C. and Michael, J. G. 2002. The relationship among organizational context, pay dispersion and managerial turnover. *Academy of Management Journal*, **45**(1): 33–42.

Boyd, R. and Richerson, P. J. (2005). *The Origin and Evolution of Cultures*. New York, NY: Oxford University Press.

Bromiley, P. and Rau, D. (2014). Towards a practice-based view of strategy. *Strategic Management Journal*, **35**: 1249–1256.

Bungay, S. (2011). *The Art of Action: How Leaders Close the Gap Between Plans, Actions and Results*. London, UK: Nicholas Brealey Publishing.

Burgelman, R. A. and Grove, A. S. (1996). Strategic dissonance. *California Management Review*, **38**(2): 8–28.

Child, J. and McGrath, R. G. (2001). Organizations unfettered: Organizational form in an information-intensive economy. *Academy of Management Journal*, **44**(6): 1135–1148.

Daft, R. and Lewin, A. (1993). Where are the theories of the new organizational forms? *Organization Science*, **4**: i–iv.

Eisenhardt, K. M. (1989). Making fast strategic decision in high-velocity environments. *Academy of Management Review*, **32**(3): 543–576.

Encyclopedia Britannica (2016). https://www.britannica.com/.

Grove, A. S. (1996). *Only the Paranoid Survive: How to Exploit the Crisis Points that Challenge Every Company and Career*. London, UK: HarperCollins Business.

Hallin, C. A. (2016). Aggregating predictions of operational uncertainties from the frontline: A new proactive risk management practice. In T. J. Andersen (ed.) *The Routledge Companion to Strategic Risk Management*. London, UK: Routledge.

Hallin, C. A. and Lind, A. S. (2016). Identification of strategic issues for crowd predictions. Paper presented at Collective Intelligence Conference: New York, NY.

Hallin, C. A., Andersen, T. J. and Tveterås, S. (2013a). Who are the better predictors: Frontline employees or executive managers? SMS 33rd Annual International Conference. Atlanta, GA: Strategic Management Society.

Hallin, C. A., Andersen, T. J. and Tveterås, S. (2013b). Fuzzy predictions for strategic decision making: A third-generation prediction market. CGSR Working Paper Series (2). Frederiksberg, Denmark: Copenhagen Business School.

Hallin, C. A., Tveterås, S. and Andersen, T. J. (2012). Judgmental forecasting of operational capabilities: Exploring a new indicator to predict financial performance. Working paper, Department of International Economics and Management. Frederiksberg, Denmark: Copenhagen Business School.

Hannan, M. T. and Freeman, J. (1989). *Organization Ecology*. Cambridge, MA: Harvard University Press.

Hong, L. and Page, S. (2001). Problem-solving by heterogeneous agents. *Journal of Economic Theory*, **97**(1): 123–63.

Hong, L. and Page, S. (2004). Groups of diverse problem solvers can outperform groups of high-ability problem solvers. *Proceedings of the National Academy of Sciences*, **101**(46): 16385–16389.

House, C. H. and Price, R. L. (2009). *The HP Phenomenon: Innovation and Business Transformation*. Stanford, CA: Stanford University Press.

Hrebiniak, L. G. (2005). *Making Strategy Work: Leading Effective Execution and Change*. Upper Saddle River, NJ: Wharton School Publishing; Pearson Education.

Kirschner, F., Paas, F. and Kirschner, P. A. (2009). A cognitive load approach to collaborative learning: United brains for complex tasks. *Educational Psychology Review*, **21**(1): 31–42.

Landemore, H. (2012). Why the many are smarter than the few and why it matters. *Journal of Public Deliberation*, **8**(1): Art. 7: 1–12.

Landemore, H. (2013). *Democratic Reason: Politics, Collective Intelligence, and the Rule of the Many*. Princeton, NJ: Princeton University Press.

Landemore, H. and Elster, J. (2012). Collective wisdom: Old and new, in H. Landemore and J. Elster (ed.) *Collective Wisdom: Principles and Mechanisms*. Cambridge, UK: Cambridge University Press.

Lovas, B. and Ghoshal, S. (2000). Strategy as guided evolution. *Strategic Management Journal*, **21**: 875–896.

Luckner, S. (2008). Prediction markets: Fundamentals, key design elements, and applications. BLED Proceedings. 21st BLED eConference eCollaboration: Overcoming Boundaries through Multi-Channel Interaction. *Association for Information Systems*.

Mackay, C. (1841). *Extraordinary Popular Delusions and the Madness of Crowds*. London, UK: Richard Bentley.

Malone, M. (2002). The H-P-Compaq Mess Isn't All Carly's Doing. *The Wall Street Journal*, May 21. Retrieved on July 25, 2016 from http://www.wsj.com/articles/SB1021933260918245440.

Malone, T. (2004). *The Future of Work. How the Order of Business will Shape our Organization, Your Management Style and Your Life*. Boston, MA: Harvard Business School Press.

Manin, B. (2005). Déliberation et discussion. *Revue Suisse de Science Politique*, **10**(4): 180–192.

McGrath, R. G. (2013). *The End of Competitive Advantage: How to Keep Your Strategy Moving as Fast as Your Business*. Boston, MA: Harvard Business Review Press.

Mintzberg, H. and Waters, J. A. (1985). Of strategies, deliberate and emergent. *Strategic Management Journal*, **6**(3): 257–272.

Mirabeau, L. and Maguire, S. (2014). From autonomous strategic behavior to emergent strategy. *Strategic Management Journal*, **35**(8): 1202–1229.

Nonaka, I., Toyama, R. and Hirata, T. (2008). *Managing Flow: A Process Theory of the Knowledge-based Firm*. Basingstoke, UK: Palgrave Macmillan.

Pascale, R. M. (1984). Perspectives on strategy: The true story behind Honda's success. *California Management Review*, **26**(3): 47–72.

Pascale, R. M. (1996). Reflections on Honda. *California Management Review*, **38**(4): 112–117.

Recanatini, F. and Ryterman, R. (2000). Disorganization or self-organization? FEEM Working Paper 26.00, World Bank.

Simons, R. (1994). How new top managers use control systems as levers of strategic renewal. *Strategic Management Journal*, **15**(3): 169–189.

Speculand, R. (2009). *Beyond Strategy: The Leader's Role in Successful Implementation*. San Francisco, CA: Jossey-Bass.

Surowiecki, J. (2004). *The Wisdom of Crowds: Why the Many are Smarter than the Few and How Collective Wisdom Shapes Business, Economies, Societies, and Nations*. New York, UK: Doubleday.

Teece, D. J. (2007). Explicating dynamic capabilities: The nature and micro-foundations of (sustainable) enterprise performance. *Strategic Management Journal*, **28**(13): 1319–1350.

Teece, D. J. (2009). *Dynamic Capabilities and Strategic Management: Organizing for Innovation and Growth*. New York, NY: Oxford University Press.

Ticoll, D. (2004). Get Self-Organized. *Harvard Business Review*, September.

Volberda, H. W. (1998). *Building the Flexible Firm*. Oxford, UK: Oxford University Press.

Wolfers, J. and Zitzewitz, E. (2004). Prediction Markets. Working Paper No. 10504. U.S. National Bureau of Economic Research.

INDEX